Colin Evans, King's

# Uneven Regional Change in Britain

## A. R. Townsend
Reader in Geography, University of Durham

CAMBRIDGE
UNIVERSITY PRESS

0521408709

Published by the Press Syndicate of the University of Cambridge
The Pitt Building, Trumpington Street, Cambridge CB2 1RP
40 West 20th Street, New York, NY 10011–4211, USA
10 Stamford Road, Oakleigh, Melbourne 3166, Australia

First published 1993

Printed in Great Britain at the University Press, Cambridge

A catalogue record for this book is available from the British Library

ISBN 0 521 40870 9 paperback

**Acknowledgements**
The publisher would like to thank the following for permission to reproduce illustrations:

Sefton Photo Library, Manchester pp. 5, 33 (bottom), 47, 78, 83; Mary Evans Picture
Library p. 13; Steve Benbow/Impact Photos p. 15; Hulton-Deutsch Collection p. 21;
Edifice/Sally Ann Norman p. 29; Edifice/Gillian Darley p. 33 (top); by courtesy of Cadbury
Ltd p. 37 (top); by courtesy of ICI p. 37 (bottom); by courtesy of Ford Motor Co. Ltd
p. 42; Peter Arkell/Impact Photos p. 49; John Sims/Impact Photos p. 58; by courtesy of
Halifax Building Society p. 60; Jon Lister/Impact Photos p. 64; Tick Ahearn p. 72; Brian
E. Rybolt/Impact Photos p. 75; Mike McQueen/Impact Photos p. 76; Philip Gordon/
Impact Photos p. 81; John Cole/Impact Photos p. 89.

The following items are based on Crown Copyright material, and are reproduced
with the permission of the Controller of Her Majesty's Stationery Office: Figs 7.4, 8.2
and Tables 7.2, 8.1.

# Contents

# Preface

In the past geographers argued that different regions of a country were likely to be different in *kind*. In Britain, some of those differences underlie the present-day map of regional variation, but today that is notably a matter of variations of *degree*. Greater prosperity in southern regions is evoked by better housing, better-stocked superstores and bigger traffic jams than in the north. The legacy of a decade of 'de-industrialisation', in derelict sites of the northern cities, is slowly being built over, but levels of employment, health and education generally remain lower in the northern regions.

This book aims to provide an introduction to regional variations in Britain in the 1990s that is easily accessible to both sixth-form students and first-year undergraduates studying the subject as part of a more general course. The book accepts that there is a tendency in different countries toward the development of marked differences in prosperity between different regions. This book summarises this body of theory and integrates it with a new summary of British industrial location history and evidence from individual firms. It studies the impact of recession in the 1930s and 1980s and the widening of the 'north–south divide'. With a framework of new maps for the period 1971–91, it analyses the 'de-industrialisation' of northern factory areas and the growth of office activity in the south, and concludes with the view that rural areas of the south of Britain have the best future today. This is despite the problems of unemployment in the south that have arisen, at the time of writing, in the recession which started in 1989. In reality, there is a need to follow the map of prosperity at county as well as at regional level, which is the practice in the last two chapters.

I am most grateful to the editors of the series and to Miss Hope Page for comments on the manuscript; to Dorothy Trotter for typing the manuscript; and to staff of the National Online Manpower Information System (referred to throughout the text as *NOMIS*) in my department for the ready availability of up-to-date statistics.

Alan Townsend
Department of Geography
University of Durham

# 1 Introduction

It is differences between places that lie at the heart of geography, and of this book on the United Kingdom. Differences can take many forms. Landforms are mostly changeless within the human life-span, and it is only recently that the public have thought that climate could change within an individual person's life-span. Many features of human geography undergo only gradual change over the centuries. The street maps of old towns are remarkably persistent, as indeed are many village and property boundaries.

The prime interest of the geographer is in today's people and patterns, and in the processes which have made them what they are. Many of these human processes of change can have significant effects within a lifetime. In the first half of this century, for example, the West Midlands industrial area, with its steelworks and growing motor industry, became the dominant area in the country's economy; today it is losing its place to cities with a greater diversity of office jobs and light industry, especially those of the south like Bristol. So too the older industrial towns of northern France have lost pride of place for growth to areas like the Rhône Valley. We can go further and see such variations as part of repeated changes in the relative wealth of the regions of Europe.

Walsall power station in the West Midlands. Walsall was once the heart of 'the Black Country'.

The purpose of this book is to understand how the geography of today's British regions arises from change. At different times in the last 200 years, the enterprise of people in different areas has yielded varying success, in agriculture, industry or services. The process of uneven regional change comprises greater increases in the value of production in some areas than others. It accelerated with the Agricultural and Industrial Revolutions of the nineteenth century. In the same way that the German economy overtook Britain's around the turn of the century, and then the USA overtook them both, the regions of Britain saw repeated changes in their league table of growth and prosperity. In the second half of the nineteenth century, for example, it appeared that rapidly-growing shipbuilding areas around Newcastle upon Tyne, Glasgow and Belfast had eclipsed London in growth and prosperity; for instance, there are recorded examples of Thames shipyards closing in the face of the new competition, and, in some cases, moving north. In turn, however, the twentieth century saw persistent growth of the economy of London, first in factories, then in the renewed growth of different kinds of office activities, before this finally passed to the adjoining regions.

These constant changes require a view of today's 'problem regions' as the outcome of varying past processes, which were often to do with the arrival of new products on world markets, or of new ways of making them. In British newspapers and television programmes, the most familiar and the simplest geographical distinction is the 'north–south divide'. Many readers would be able to interpret this in terms of the replacement of 'old, heavy industries like coal, shipbuilding and steel of several northern regions' by 'the growth of light industry and offices in London and the south'. These are, none the less, very general descriptions and explanations. It is the task in this book to measure regional economic differences in a precise way and to explain past and present regional change in terms of increasing levels of detail.

### Units of study

The United Kingdom, as the subject of this book, comprises England, Wales, Scotland and Northern Ireland. These have precise boundaries, and for some purposes the last three have their own government departments. However, England is largest by far, especially in terms of the size of its population, and is normally divided into eight *Standard Regions*. With the three 'countries' this provides 11 units of study, adopted for this book's main series of maps. So it is valuable to identify them clearly. This is done in Fig. 1.1 with reference to their principal cities and subdivisions. In the text, these regions are identified by capital letters (e.g. 'East Midlands'). In England and Wales the 'building blocks' of the regions are counties, whose identity and boundaries were revised in 1974, and reconsidered again from 1990 onwards.

Geographers commonly think of two principal kinds of region:

1 The *functional region* relies on one dominant centre for its principal office services and specialist supplies.
2 The *formal region* is notable for common characteristics – for example relief, or density of population – across its area, which also distinguish it from its neighbours (it may fall across parts of several functional regions).

In this century geographers and governments have tended to recognise English regional centres at Newcastle upon Tyne, Leeds, Manchester, Birmingham, Bristol and London, together with Nottingham and Norwich. Figure 1.1 shows how the eight English statistical regions comprise groups of counties surrounding these eight centres.

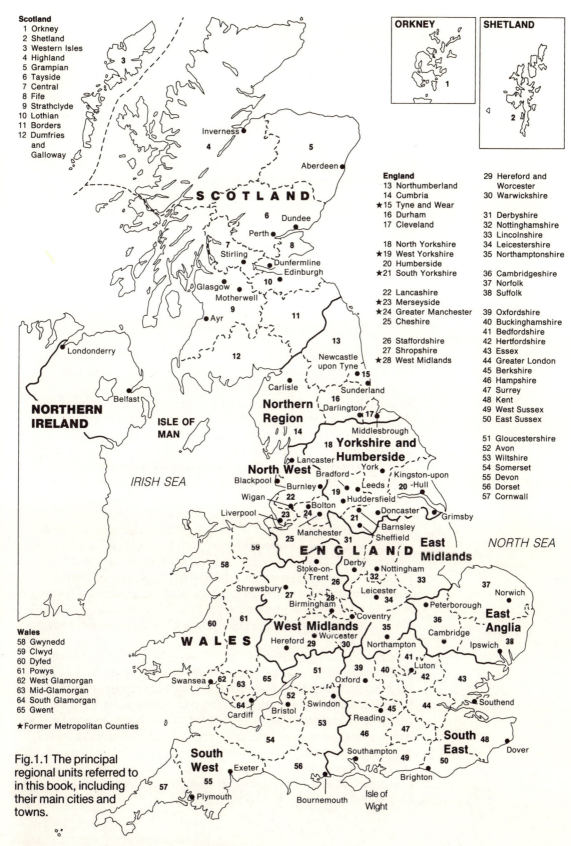

**Scotland**
1 Orkney
2 Shetland
3 Western Isles
4 Highland
5 Grampian
6 Tayside
7 Central
8 Fife
9 Strathclyde
10 Lothian
11 Borders
12 Dumfries
   and
   Galloway

**ORKNEY**

**SHETLAND**

Inverness

Aberdeen

**SCOTLAND**

Dundee

Perth

Stirling

Dunfermline
Edinburgh

Glasgow

Motherwell

Ayr

**England**
13 Northumberland
14 Cumbria
★15 Tyne and Wear
16 Durham
17 Cleveland

18 North Yorkshire
★19 West Yorkshire
20 Humberside
★21 South Yorkshire

22 Lancashire
★23 Merseyside
★24 Greater Manchester
25 Cheshire

26 Staffordshire
27 Shropshire
★28 West Midlands

29 Hereford and
   Worcester
30 Warwickshire

31 Derbyshire
32 Nottinghamshire
33 Lincolnshire
34 Leicestershire
35 Northamptonshire

36 Cambridgeshire
37 Norfolk
38 Suffolk

39 Oxfordshire
40 Buckinghamshire
41 Bedfordshire
42 Hertfordshire
43 Essex
44 Greater London
45 Berkshire
46 Hampshire
47 Surrey
48 Kent
49 West Sussex
50 East Sussex

51 Gloucestershire
52 Avon
53 Wiltshire
54 Somerset
55 Devon
56 Dorset
57 Cornwall

Londonderry

Belfast

**NORTHERN
IRELAND**

**ISLE OF
MAN**

Newcastle
upon Tyne

Carlisle

Sunderland

**Northern
Region**
Darlington

Middlesbrough

**IRISH SEA**

**Yorkshire and
Humberside**

Lancaster

York

**North West**

Bradford

Kingston-upon
-Hull

Blackpool

Burnley

Leeds

Wigan

Huddersfield

Liverpool

Bolton

Doncaster

Manchester

Barnsley

Grimsby

**NORTH SEA**

Sheffield

**East
Midlands**

**E N G L A N D**

Stoke-on-
Trent

Derby

Nottingham

Shrewsbury

Peterborough

Norwich

**East
Anglia**

Birmingham

Leicester

Coventry

Cambridge

Ipswich

**West Midlands**

Worcester

Hereford

Northampton

**WALES**

Luton

**Wales**
58 Gwynedd
59 Clwyd
60 Dyfed
61 Powys
62 West Glamorgan
63 Mid-Glamorgan
64 South Glamorgan
65 Gwent

Swansea

Oxford

Southend

Swindon

Cardiff

Bristol

Reading

**South
East**

Dover

**South
West**

Southampton

Brighton

★Former Metropolitan Counties

Exeter

Plymouth

Bournemouth

Isle of
Wight

Fig.1.1 The principal
regional units referred to
in this book, including
their main cities and
towns.

Some regions may be said to be *functional*. Thus in the South East and West Midlands, London and Birmingham respectively have no rivals as the regional centres. In the South West, several counties are far distant from the city of Bristol, and the region is more *formal*. In the North West, Manchester has achieved dominance over Liverpool after the decline of its port activity. Strong rivalry also exists within Scotland, with Glasgow, the former industrial port, challenging Edinburgh's role in office growth, services and leisure. Belfast, also an industrial port, is absolutely dominant within Northern Ireland. Cardiff, however, exerts little influence in the northern half of Wales, except as the centre of Welsh official government business; rather than being a functional region, Wales in fact constitutes a classic formal region, based on common features of relief, history, language and agriculture. Most of the 11 units have elements of both kinds of region. Their boundaries may only approximately meet the needs of this kind of geographical analysis; indeed, there is a need for a more fine-grained emphasis on the distinction of urban and rural (see Chapter 8).

**Measuring regional economic differences**

A wide range of statistics is available for these 11 units. What are the best measures for comparing their levels of success in the world?

In the same way that the size of a country's economy can be measured, so too can that of a region. The value of total output is the most obvious measure; in both cases it may be defined to include the value both of physical goods produced in the area and of services supplied in and from the area. However, countries and regions vary in size; the normal way to compare them is to divide the value of output of each by its total population. This yields a figure of 'production per head'.

Using this measure, it is possible to compare the relative levels of output in our 11 units of the UK. In Fig.1.2 the height of each bar is proportional to production per head (the UK average is shown as 100). The greatest evident contrast lies between the South East, as a large region of relatively high income, and the other extreme of Northern Ireland, an area of surprisingly low population and income. This range of about 60 per cent in production per head between areas is relatively low compared with the range in some other European Community countries.

In general, a comparison of Figs 1.1 and 1.2 shows a north–south divide in income levels, with all the regions falling below 95 per cent of the UK average lying in the north and west. Many other sets of figures show a similar pattern. In general, government taxation of income and profits bears proportionately more heavily on richer people and regions, and less on poorer; therefore, differences in 'take-home pay' – that is, what families actually can spend – are somewhat less than those shown in Fig.1.2. None the less, the pattern of variation has withstood a number of influences, including government policies to try and eliminate it over more than half a century.

Fig.1.2 The value of regional production per head, as percentages of the UK average (1989 = 100). Official data for 'gross domestic product per capita'.

*Source: Regional Trends*, HMSO, 1991.

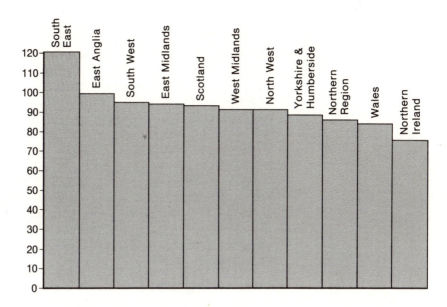

## Uneven change over time

Economists have often assumed that the operation of the free market works 'towards equilibrium' – that is, that differences in, say, prices quoted for a given product will iron themselves out. One view of the relations of regions over time is that, with a free market in labour, capital and technology allowing these factors of production to flow readily between them, flows of these items will eliminate regional economic differences. For instance, labour and capital will move from an underemployed region, where they are underused, to one of greater prosperity. Thus the greater prosperity of England over much of this century has led to the familiar feature of migrant families moving from Scotland, Ireland and Wales. Over more extensive periods of time it is easier to assess the relative growth of regions through trends like migration than through historical figures for production per head.

If perfect equilibrium had been achieved, say between England and Scotland, then the supply of workers and of jobs in each area would be in balance, and there would be no *net* migration flow between them. In fact, the main point of this book is that such inter-regional balances are never attained. Rather, a whole set of human experience and evidence bears witness to abiding imbalance as the expression of relationships between regions (Table 1.1).

**Table 1.1   Human evidence of regional imbalance**

| Poorer/declining region | Richer/growing region |
| --- | --- |
| High rates of unemployment | Labour shortage |
| Low 'economic activity rates' | High 'economic activity rates' |
| Net outward migration | Net inward migration |
| Declining population | Growing population |
| Surplus housing and service facilities | Pressure on housing and services |

9

A period of growth in one region can rely only so far for extra workers on a higher 'economic activity rate'; that is the proportion of the population of working age which is at work. An increase in activity rates is commonly achieved through greater proportions of women 'participating' in the labour force. Beyond a certain point, net inward migration occurs, particularly from poorer/declining regions. These latter areas can be identified by high rates of unemployment, measured as the number of people seeking work divided by those who are 'economically active'. Thus human problems can be seen as a feature left over from a period of decline.

The history of the British Isles in the last 300 years shows that balance has rarely been achieved; at any one time, at least one region has usually shown marked growth, and several have been declining. Of course, the identities of the two kinds have changed over the long and medium term. Since the Industrial Revolution we can identify three phases:

1 Before 1921, different *coalfields*, which are in Scotland, Wales, the north of England and the Midlands, experienced rapid industrialisation at different times.
2 From the 1920s to the 1970s, an *axial belt* of greater prosperity, from London to Birmingham, Manchester and Leeds (inclusive), contrasted with conditions of decline in the *peripheral coalfields*, such as south Wales.
3 In the 1980s, *the north–south divide* was more in evidence; even remoter areas of the south gained in prosperity, while the North West, Yorkshire and Humberside and the West Midlands came to share high unemployment with the more peripheral coalfields of the north.

Fig.1.3 Changing regional shares of the total population of Great Britain, 1801–1991.

Figure 1.3 shows the changing shares of different present-day regions in the total population of the UK. Since 1801, the outstanding feature is that the nineteenth-century industrial growth of the north proves to have been only a passing phase. So there have been two reversals of the economic advantages enjoyed by UK regions. The dominant area for population, farming, trade and politics before the Industrial Revolution – the greater South East – has again won a large share of national growth in the closing decades of the twentieth century. It is necessary now to explore the reasons for such changes.

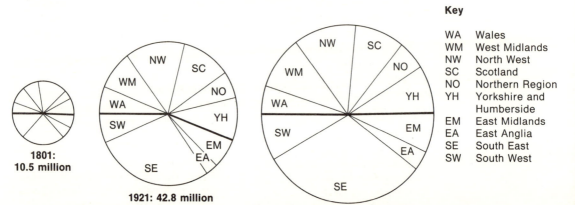

1801: 10.5 million

1921: 42.8 million

1991: 55.7 million

**Key**

WA  Wales
WM  West Midlands
NW  North West
SC  Scotland
NO  Northern Region
YH  Yorkshire and Humberside
EM  East Midlands
EA  East Anglia
SE  South East
SW  South West

# 2    Understanding pre-war patterns

There are two reasons for taking studies of industrial location back
before the two World Wars. Firstly, they show how individual places,
their work and their society, result from unending processes of change
at work since the Industrial Revolution. Secondly, they indicate how
capital is constantly searching out new channels of and areas for
investment, and withdraws from previous ones, sometimes gradually,
sometimes suddenly. These processes are most likely to be still at work
and help an understanding of the relative fate of different regions now
and in the future.

Britain's industrial growth, unlike that of most other countries, was
not organised by central government. The unplanned nature of
investment in the emerging economic system produced regional
diversity and regional imbalance; that is, inequalities in development
between geographical areas. The story was not always straightforward.
There were many false starts, setbacks and complexities in the evolution
of the changing map of economic activity. Much of the early progress in
specific areas stemmed from technical inventions and their interplay
with physical resources as they spread, or 'diffused', to other areas. Yet
the Industrial Revolution itself started with radical, if gradual, change.

## The obsolescence of dispersed patterns of industry

### Market location

The well-established eighteenth-century pattern of market towns and
villages might be seen by many geographers as the major locational
attraction for entrepreneurs, both those making and those selling goods.
Costs of transport over any great distance were high, so goods were
generally made near the market for them; hence there was a fairly even
geographical distribution of producers of each class of goods. Yet
successive waves of concentration on coalfields and ports left the
average town with little industry, except for particular trades such as
brewing, where high transport costs kept the making of beer close to the
market, and baking, where the importance of freshness made for the
limited distribution areas which survived until recently.

### Early locational obsolescence

Concentration in specialised producing areas, on the other hand, had an
early start. Some of the places in which industries were concentrated in
earlier times are little known today, because those older industries have
disappeared or have been hidden by later 'layers' of investment. Figure
2.1 shows the eighteenth-century pattern, including, for instance, busy
areas of the woollen industry in East Anglia, particularly around the city
of Norwich, and in the South West, in Gloucestershire, Wiltshire,

11

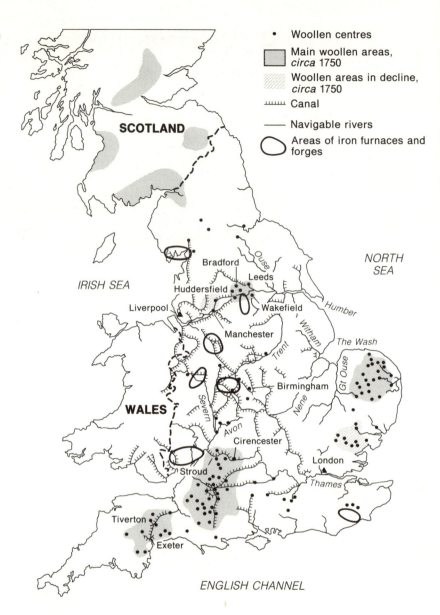

Fig.2.1 British industry in the eighteenth century.

*Source: Cambridge Modern History Atlas* (1970) Cambridge University Press, Cambridge, p. 97.

**Legend:**

- • Woollen centres
- ▨ Main woollen areas, *circa* 1750
- ░ Woollen areas in decline, *circa* 1750
- ⊔⊔⊔ Canal
- — Navigable rivers
- ◯ Areas of iron furnaces and forges

Map labels: SCOTLAND, NORTH SEA, IRISH SEA, Bradford, Leeds, Huddersfield, Liverpool, Wakefield, Manchester, Ouse, Humber, The Wash, Gt Ouse, Birmingham, Witham, Trent, Nene, WALES, Severn, Avon, Cirencester, London, Stroud, Thames, Tiverton, Exeter, ENGLISH CHANNEL

Devon and Somerset. Most Scottish towns had textile work, again based on local wool production, some of which survived to this century. For the most part, however, by the mid-nineteenth century the textile industry of southern England had been overtaken by cottage and eventually factory production in West Yorkshire.

It has been increasingly realised that the Industrial Revolution came only gradually to the different regions of Britain. Water mills along the fast-flowing streams of Shropshire from the early eighteenth century were only gradually replaced by coal-powered factories. The effective arrival of the factory system dates from the late eighteenth century, when cotton spinning in the southern Pennines, notably in Lancashire, began to be transferred from workers' homes to water-powered mills. Although some of these mills were still in fairly remote valleys and later closed, around Manchester they provided one of the first bases of regional concentration.

In the early part of the Industrial Revolution, water was the source of power for industry. The ironworks at Coalbrookdale, seen here later, when coal was used as well, was one of the first centres of industrial development (Shropshire).

## Nineteenth-century concentration of industry

### 'Agglomeration'

As the world's first industrial country, by 1850 half of Britain's population lived in towns. People moved from the countryside and the obsolete industrial areas to new centres of population in each region. As most of the new industrial towns were in the north, we can talk of 'a drift to the north' and of 'rural–urban migration'.

As to why concentration should occur at all, it is of value to introduce here the term 'agglomeration', used by the German theorist Weber. The concept refers to the advantages of clustering economic activity in a densely occupied area. This generates economies – that is, reductions in the cost of a unit of production – in three ways. Firstly, a firm can achieve *economies of scale* by concentrating its own production at one point; hence the profitability of the factory system under Victorian capitalism. Secondly, firms in a given industry may, in certain situations, achieve *localisation economies* by locating near to other firms in that industry; they may engage in complementary tasks, and enjoy the benefits of a common pool of skilled labour and of specialised services provided, for instance, by banks or railway companies. Thirdly, all industries in a single area may benefit from general *urbanisation economies*, arising from the economies of scale of the large urban unit such as in providing housing, roads, education, shopping, leisure and public services, for industries of all kinds.

### Coalfield agglomeration

The particular locations of new growth and agglomeration in nineteenth-century Britain were virtually all on or close to coalfields. By 1800 the steam engine had been modified to drive machinery, and the importance of coal increased rapidly from that time. However, calculations show that transport costs from the mine to a cotton mill or a blast furnace were prohibitively expensive over more than about 10 kilometres. In turn, *localisation economies* were very evident, as individual coalfields each specialised in a different use for coal, whether in iron works, pottery manufacture, textiles, other trades, or exports. At first sight, therefore, the map of Victorian industrial Britain (Fig. 2.2) is of a highly ordered and predictable kind. The relative costs of transporting raw materials and fuel to alternative factory locations, and finished goods to market, would normally produce large-scale development in coalfield subregions.

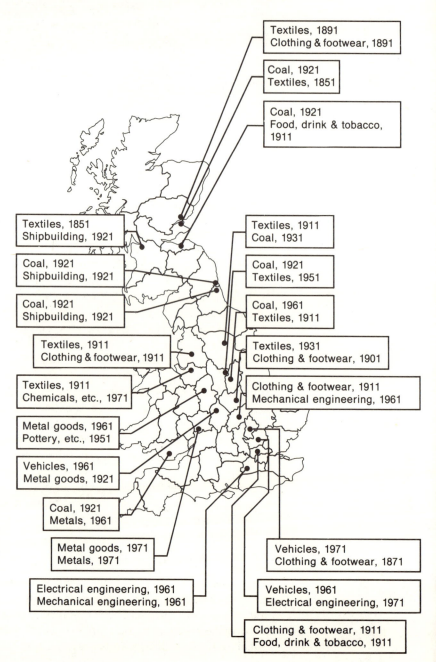

Fig.2.2 Specialised industrial areas. Industries with highest and second highest peak employment levels in the ten-yearly census, 1841–1971 (excluding areas with highest peak in agriculture).

*Source:* Lee, C.H. (1979) *British Regional Employment Statistics, 1841–1971*, Cambridge University Press, Cambridge.

However, the simple picture painted by past generations of textbooks breaks down as our knowledge of the nineteenth century is more carefully analysed. Firstly, many of the industrial specialisms of the different coalfields were effectively decided *before* coal began to be used in those industries; the origins of Lancashire and Yorkshire textiles lie in the underemployment of farm households and their need to take up domestic crafts. Secondly, textbooks have tended to attribute the industrial specialism of a coalfield to its other resources – iron ore or pottery clay, for example – ignoring the fact that resources such as these were widely available in many different coalfields, and were not peculiar to those that happened to specialise in iron and steel making, or in pottery. Thirdly, changes occurred over time in the relative strength of different coalfields in the same specialism, for instance iron and steel. Lastly, in some cases one specialism was succeeded by another that was more advantageous; thus Fig. 2.2 shows how Strathclyde specialised in cotton textiles until after the mid-nineteenth century, and then switched its resources to metal shipbuilding, clearly one of the heavy industries which could not be undertaken on an inland coalfield. However, extreme specialisation was not a universal advantage. Strathclyde did retain a variety of industries, the West Midlands continually evolved a wide range of metal products, and Greater Manchester and West Yorkshire had diversified into the full range of industry by the early twentieth century.

Terraced housing for coal miners in the Rhondda Valley of South Wales.

Nor was the supply of transport necessarily the crucial factor in regional development that it is sometimes made out to be. The growth of the canal network after 1760 and of the main railway network after 1830 are sometimes seen as 'causes' of the Industrial Revolution. In fact, many of the canals were primarily of use only within their respective regions, and railways, being *part of* the Revolution, were commonly built *well after* the growth of manufacturing or mining, to provide transport to pre-existing industrial centres; for instance, the Liverpool and Manchester Railway of 1830, or the Manchester and Leeds of 1845. Transport was soon a plentiful rather than a scarce resource. Thus individual railway companies *competed* to reach and serve the coalfield areas, as well as the other leading cities and ports. Figure 2.3 demonstrates how large rural areas were held by individual Victorian railway companies as monopoly zones, from which they built competitive lines to reach the coalfields and leading cities, such as Leicester, or ports such as Hull. The Yorkshire/Derbyshire/Nottinghamshire coalfield was served by no less than seven of the railways that existed before 1922.

**Railway companies and the areas they monopolised (simplified)**

| | |
|---|---|
| CAM | Cambrian |
| CR | Caledonian |
| FR | Furness |
| GCR | Great Central |
| GER | Great Eastern |
| GNOSR | Great North of Scotland |
| GNR | Great Northern |
| GSWR | Glasgow & South Western |
| GWR | Great Western |
| HR | Highland |
| LBSCR | London, Brighton & South Coast |
| LNWR | London & North Western |
| LSWR | London & South Western |
| L&Y | Lancashire & Yorkshire |
| MR | Midland |
| NBR | North British |
| NER | North Eastern |
| NSR | North Staffordshire |
| SECR | South Eastern & Chatham |

**Number of independent railways serving:**

3 ▨ Coalfields

③ Other cities and ports

Fig.2.3 The attraction of private railway companies to coalfield areas, other principal cities and leading ports, before 1922.

## Non-coalfield development

Railway companies themselves were heavily involved in the promotion of specific types of towns which developed away from the coalfields. The new seaside resorts such as Blackpool (Lancashire) and Skegness (Lincolnshire) often lay on the nearest coastline to their respective coalfield cities, and were assisted by cheap fares and railway promotion. The new railway engineering towns, such as Crewe (Cheshire) and Swindon (Wiltshire), were conveniently placed within the networks of the companies that built them. Most new port development had railway involvement, for instance in the Great Central Railway's development of Grimsby, and certain new industries grew up at the 'break-of-bulk point' for manufacturing of imported goods; for instance, food processing could economically take place at Liverpool, Hull or Bristol. There were some additional industrial areas, for instance the traditional straw hat industry of Luton (Bedfordshire) which did not reach its peak employment until 1871 (Fig. 2.2), and the Northamptonshire footwear industry. With these exceptions, all marked industrial growth occurred on or very close to coalfields, and later on from 1850 to 1930 on or near the iron ore fields of Cleveland, Lincolnshire and Northamptonshire. Some large towns and cities like Preston and Derby which happened to lie just off the coalfields were linked with them by less than 10 kilometres of rail and shared fully in their growth.

## Variation over time: 'long waves'

The uneven regional development of the nineteenth century can therefore be reduced to a number of spatial generalisations, which all relate to Weber's concept of agglomeration and, in a general way, to the minimisation of transport costs. If we looked in a little more detail we could find extensive variations between industrial areas in their use of labour and their rates of growth at different times. Some areas relied at an early stage on the labour of women and children; in their peak years of employment (as recorded in national censuses), the textile industries (Fig. 2.2) in Tayside, Strathclyde, Lancashire, Cheshire, the West Riding of Yorkshire and Leicestershire relied on females for more than half their workforce, while mining at that time employed virtually no women.

A further feature of Fig. 2.2 is that the different leading industrial sectors of areas peaked in very different census years. The figure shows, for each area, which industry had the highest level of employment in any census of population between 1841 and 1971 (the 'runner-up' is also shown). The outstanding feature is that virtually all the peaks fell in the four censuses, 1911, 1921, 1961 and 1971. Passing their peak in the twentieth century indicates the eventual onset of decline of specialised industrial areas, but it may also be seen as part of an identified *50-year cycle* in the dynamics of the world industrial economy. The concept of such a cycle can lead us back, remarkably, to the view that there was not one 'Industrial Revolution', but several. Kondratieff, a Russian economist writing in the 1920s, had identified up to then three waves of expansion and contraction based on movements of commodity prices since the late eighteenth century. The first of these coincided with the 'Industrial Revolution' in Britain after 1790; the second saw rival growth in Europe after the 1840s leading eventually to the 'Victorian depression' of 1893/94; while the third coincided with the imperialist expansion of Britain and Germany, reaching its climax in 1914. If Kondratieff had lived, he might well have forecast recovery from the 1930s to the mid-1960s.

The pattern of 50-year cycles is generally agreed, but not whether they result from or are caused by technological changes. To the geographer, what is interesting is that each new wave, associated with steam power, railway development and steel-making from the 1840s to 1870s, or with chemicals from the 1890s to 1920s, involved a different set of countries and of regions within countries. Thus we can associate the arrival of distinct new industrial areas with new products (Fig. 2.4); for instance, between the 'Victorian depression' and the 'Imperialist boom', the growth of the chemicals industries of Cheshire or Cleveland, or the arrival of 'replacement industries' such as motor manufacture in the West Midlands.

What is important for our present study is to see how regional development proceeded through marked impulses of growth and pauses in growth. Clearly, an industrial landscape that has evolved from the canal era of 1800 may still be very different today from, say, 'a new town' like Middlesbrough which took off in the 1850s. But we can witness not only selective regional growth, but also selective regional decline. Some industrial areas which grew in one 'upswing' (Fig. 2.4)

17

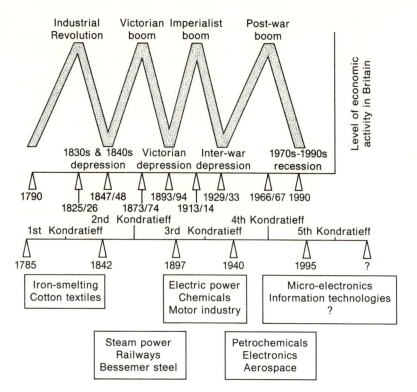

Fig.2.4 A schematic representation of innovation cycles and long waves of economic activity.

*Source:* Healey and Ilbery (1990) *Location and Change*, Oxford University Press, Oxford, p.15. Reproduced by permission of Oxford University Press.

declined markedly *in a later one*. An early eighteenth-century area like Shropshire fell into relative decline as early as the 1850s. By the twentieth century, regions such as South Wales fell into absolute decline, typically in the downswings of Kondratieff long waves after the First World War and after the peak activity of the mid-1960s. Some authors have written not only about locational obsolescence but also about 'gales of creative destruction' in which financiers withdraw capital from industries with declining profits and transfer the money to investments in new industries, technologies, regions and countries. Having recognised the possibilities of regional expansion and decline, the concern in the rest of this book is how they have inter-related in this century.

## 'Layers of investment' across the map of Britain

We have already seen how production areas of the eighteenth century were often replaced by new regions with a new technology in the nineteenth. We have also seen how 'replacement industries' might take up the resources and investments of a given region to make a different product in the same area. In either case, technological, economic and social change may be considerable between the first investment period and the second; the gap is typically marked by at least one long 'downswing' cycle. The gap can be long enough to indicate that we are dealing with a different set of investment needs which yields different patterns of costs and advantages. In short, the factors of industrial location will have changed over time between half-century periods of investment.

It is suggested here that these are differences not merely of degree, but of kind. Although many basic principles remain the same, the concept of one overall all-purpose location theory must be rejected. The cost and revenue structure of industry changes too much over time. Thus Table 2.1 attempts to show the different ways in which factors combine to produce effectively different subregional patterns in different periods. The purpose here is not by any means to remove the element of human choice, or 'behavioural variability'. Rather it is to generalise with the purpose of understanding which kinds of subregion benefited most in different periods from new industry. Of course there are always exceptions to a prevailing pattern. Certain tourist areas have seen a revival of craft industry in the recent past, but most people would see crafts as essentially a pre-industrial feature in Britain.

**Table 2.1   The changing nature of industrial location factors**

| Dominant factor | Dominant period of location in industrialised world | | |
|---|---|---|---|
| | Approx. dates | UK subregional examples | Foreign examples |
| 9  General 'de-industrialisation' | 1975 ongoing | Steelworks closures: most subregions | Heavy engineering: southern Belgium |
| 8  National and multinational 'spatial division of labour' | 1965 ongoing | US-owned electronics: Central Scotland | US-owned electronics: Taiwan |
| 7  Regional dispersal: 'urban–rural shift' | 1955 ongoing | Light industry: Devon | Electronics: rural New England |
| 6  National dispersal: often to labour reserves under 'regional policy' | 1945–75 | Car production: Merseyside | Steelworks development: southern Italy |
| 5  Strategic dispersal by government | 1935–45 | Ordnance factories: County Durham | Ordnance factories: southern Germany |
| 4  Market orientation | 1920–40 | Domestic appliances: West London | Engineering: Milan |
| 3  Weight of heavy materials and/or fuel | 1800–1920 | Iron and steel: West Midlands | Heavy engineering: German Ruhr |
| 2  Water power | 1750–1800 | Textiles: Greater Manchester | Textiles: Switzerland |
| 1  Craft industry | To 18th century | Many towns | Many towns |

Table 2.1 is deliberately arranged like a 'stratigraphical column' in geology, reflecting the way in which layers of deposition are superimposed on each other. Of course, we are not normally talking about continuous layers of factories. It is possible to think, however, about a complete map showing the variation of industrial costs. On this 'cost-surface', represented by the map of Britain at various dates, industry will choose to locate in subregions of different attributes. However, in the lowest layer, of 'craft industry', production was relatively widespread, as it used different local raw materials to provide for basic needs of goods in different local markets. The nineteenth-century Luton hat industry was an isolated survival from this period. By contrast, the growth of industrial water-power was, as stated, concentrated in areas like the valleys of the Pennines. In the next (the most important) entry, the 'weight of heavy materials and/or fuel' is

seen as the crucial factor in minimising total transport costs by location of manufacturing at particular points in a coalfield region, an area of raw materials, a market or an intervening port region. The relative pull of these three locations is reconciled by calculation of freight transport costs, broadly as in Weber's models. These three rows of Table 2.1 encapsulate most of the locational concepts we have observed so far. In fact, the period suggested for the last heading, 1800–1920, is comparatively long. There were marked new developments in the later nineteenth-century 'upswings', including, naturally, the use of coalfield ports for shipbuilding, and the profitability of bringing coal to new steelworks in the iron-bearing areas of Lincolnshire and Northamptonshire.

In developing the concept of 'layers' of industry, Massey (1984) stressed that the attraction of new investment, and the form it took, might be affected by the features surviving in an area from previous layers of investment. Thus an area's past practices on whether or not to employ women, to rely on shift-working, or to develop peaceful industrial relations, might attract or deter particular kinds of investors. In general, characteristics once established might be long-lasting. It should be noted, however, that trading links between older and newer industries ('economies of localisation') are not very common. The most frequent pattern is that 'male' and 'female' industries, heavy and light, or old and new, simply share the same facilities through 'economies of urbanisation'. For example, in this century clothing and textile industries have commonly moved to areas of heavy, male-employing industry in order to recruit female workers.

## National market orientation

The biggest change in the nature of industrial location occurred after the First World War with the rejection of the northern coalfields in favour of the southern-biased *national* market. In the second half of the nineteenth century, improved transport had freed industry to a limited extent from the coalfields, and 'a drift to the south' had been noted before the First World War, albeit masked by high employment levels of the 1911 census in traditional industrial areas. In the West Midlands coalfield, the motor vehicle industry had taken root as a 'replacement industry' by 1914.

> In the Black Country engineering traditions developed on a coalfield which was well on the way to extinction. They might as well have developed off the coalfields altogether . . . alike on active coalfields, on worked-out coalfields and on no coalfield at all, therefore, the new engineering industries were rapidly evolving . . . what was important, of course, was not coal or the lack of it, but the existence of an industrial tradition that could be transmuted: most commonly the coalfields had thrown up such a tradition, but it could readily evolve in a different environment.
>
> Hall (1976) pp. 413–14.

It was otherwise the pull of the national market which made itself felt in the 1920s and 1930s (Table 2.1), when industry was gradually freed from the coalfields. Many towns had local electricity supplies, but the key factor was the establishment of the national electric power grid in 1926, which largely equalised power costs between regions. The expanding industries of the day were motor vehicles, electrical engineering, chemicals and pharmaceuticals, and most showed a clear preference not for resource-based locations, but for areas such as west London, Oxford or the West Midlands, producing a new kind of broad concentration near the centre of the *national* market.

The lesson of such proximity to markets was not necessarily that it reduced production costs, but that it increased revenue, and therefore net profits, in a number of ways. Firstly, several of the new products, for example radios or pharmaceuticals, were at the time luxury items, which depended on the spread of international fashions through London and in the wealthiest national income groups as potential customers. Secondly, marketing relied on personal contacts in the most lucrative purchasing areas, together with after-sales service. Lastly, important sectors, including defence, electronics and aircraft manufacture, depended on contact with purchasing departments of government in London.

## The 'axial belt' and the 'periphery'

Thus in Britain new industry tended to concentrate near the centre of the national market in the London–Birmingham belt (especially near London's North Circular Road), in parallel with growth around the other European national centres: Paris, Berlin and Milan. With a surprising degree of survival of London manufacturing trades, such as clothing, from the nineteenth century, and investment by businessmen in new sectors, the cumulative effects became apparent in an economic recovery in the 1930s. Between 1933 and 1937 London and the south had just over half (51 per cent) of the country's 2,565 factory openings, but under two-fifths (39 per cent) of the 2,158 closures, a net gain of 461 factories.

A queue of unemployed men outside the Wigan Labour Exchange, Lancashire, in 1939.

In the meantime, changes in the world trading pattern after the First World War caused a worsening downturn in exports of coal, steel, ships and cotton. These industries had peaked in their employment levels in 1911 or 1921, and then suffered mounting job losses in the period 1921–31 in their regions of concentration (Fig. 2.5), especially Wales, northern England and Scotland. Because of their industrial structure – the mix of industries which they inherited from the nineteenth century – it was the coastal coalfields of the 'periphery' of Britain that showed the severest levels of unemployment in 1931–32 (page 21) and which needed more time to recover and move towards prosperity in the following decade.

Assessing these changes in the 1930s, leading geographers put forward the idea of an 'axial belt' of thriving industry which spanned Greater London, the West Midlands, Greater Manchester and West Yorkshire (Fig. 2.5). The fate of the 'peripheral areas', outside the belt, rested on the nation's conscience during the Second World War. We can say that the worst problems of the north were born in the inter-war 'downswing', when decisive statistical trends demonstrated a reversal of many of the locational values of the pre-existing British map, with the distribution of consumer income replacing mineral resources as the deciding factor of change.

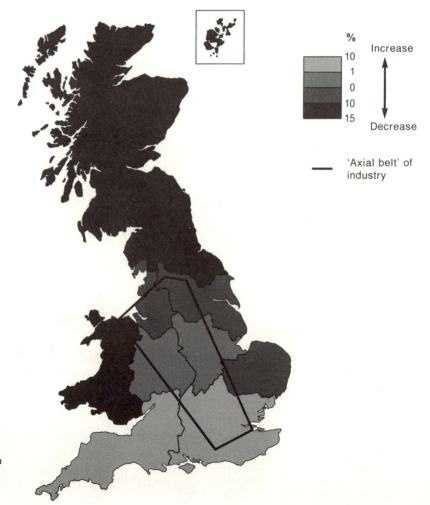

Fig.2.5 Changes in regional employment, 1921–31.

*Source:* Law, C.M. (1980) *British Regional Development since World War I*, David & Charles, Newton Abbot.

# 3 'Core' and 'periphery' as post-war themes

In the three decades following the Second World War the housing needs of city populations grew and planners had to allow urban 'overspill', either through creating New Towns or through allowing building in Green Belts. But the principal geographical issue was the *inter*-regional balance of economic growth between 'core' and 'periphery'. The spatial pattern of change was the same as before the war, showing a contrast between the growing 'axial belt', including London and Birmingham, and the depressed coalfield areas which had suffered high unemployment in the 1930s. Once established, this distinction, as we shall see, proved difficult to eradicate. Politicians did try: they were afraid of high unemployment returning to areas like Strathclyde or Tyne and Wear, and it was this fear that made them establish a counter-policy from the end of the war in 1945.

In the event the national economy developed fairly well in the post-war years. A difference certainly remained between the two kinds of area, but it was smaller than before 1939. The economic context had changed from the inter-war 'downswing' to an 'upswing' or 'long boom' in which government management of the economy assisted regular increases in production, certainly till 1966/67 (see Fig. 2.4). This meant that even the 'peripheral' coalfields were fairly fully employed in economic terms. On the other hand, in the 'axial belt' many of the resources of labour, transport and housing facilities were stretched to the limit by the demands posed by record prosperity. The general economic advantages of *agglomeration*, which had occurred through urbanisation in the London–Birmingham belt, began to be reversed. Firms became aware of urban traffic congestion, and labour shortages became severe. It is worth recalling that, even before the war, such conditions had prompted some firms to locate new production units spontaneously where more labour was available, in areas of unemployment.

## Wartime lessons of location

The significance of wartime policy itself has often been forgotten, but it further promoted the possibilities of relocation. Official orders of 1934 had classified areas of Britain into air safety zones ('safe', 'unsafe' and 'dangerous') with a view to planning the relocation of aircraft firms and all other strategic production in the less vulnerable areas, mainly in the west of the country. The effect remains visible in the presence even now of aircraft factories in Bristol, Gloucester, Greater Manchester and Lancashire. In northern regions, heavily increased wartime production of iron and steel, armaments and ships was of a temporary nature. In southern regions, spending by the wartime London government gave a permanent boost to the growth of electronics production and research. However, the government encouraged the movement to different regions of armaments factories, some of which were successfully converted to peacetime use. The government built Royal Ordnance factories, many of which continued after the war at or near Bridgend, Nottingham, Leeds, Durham and Glasgow, or were redeveloped as light industrial estates (see Table 2.1, row 5).

These are important examples of government taking part in the location of industry, public and private. It was seen that industry could be successfully moved away from London. In broader terms, *deglomeration*, as opposed to agglomeration in the London–Birmingham belt, was given support. These factors, and the strategic air threat, fed into the recommendations of wartime committees which generated post-war policy, chiefly those of the Barlow Report on the 'Distribution of the Industrial Population'.

### Regional economic imbalance: international theory

At this stage it is relevant to turn to international theory before assessing the interplay between British post-war manufacturing trends and government policy. We have seen that Britain shows a regional imbalance with two separate causes working in the same direction. In Chapter 2 it was suggested that the inter-war growth of central and southern areas of Britain was based to a considerable extent on advantages of *location*. At the same time the 'peripheral' areas happened to have the industrial *structures* which were liable to create renewed problems of decline, in their dependence on mining and heavy industry. These are different but complementary reasons for the regional imbalance inherited in 1945. Whatever the origin of such regional imbalances, there is a considerable amount of international theory as to whether, on the one hand, they are inevitable, and, on the other, they can be corrected.

Under the concepts mentioned in Chapter 1, any economic imbalance between two regions would be a temporary lapse which was bound in time to disappear. For example, an excess of labour demand in one region rather than another would be met by movement of labour in one direction, and of capital investment in the other, producing a return to 'equilibrium' between regions. A contrary view has grown up in international thought, which suggests that it is 'regional disequilibrium' that is to be expected. According to this view, an initial difference between regions will increase rather than decrease so that an imbalance between regions will be the norm, as it is between countries. Critics of the capitalist system (following neo-Marxist views) argued that 'disequilibrium' was part and parcel of that system, reflecting instability over time, periodic crises, and imbalance between areas, all shown by Britain in the 1930s and 1980s. The accumulation of investment in one area might exhaust its temporary advantages (of resources, labour supply, housing, etc.) and hinder later phases of expansion, which would be moved elsewhere to maintain profits.

### 'Cumulative causation'

The general consensus of international views has stressed not only that agglomeration in one area of a country is common, but that it works to the detriment of the others. An important family of models is based on the concept of 'cumulative causation'. This suggests that growth attracts more growth. Once a region is growing more rapidly than the rest of the country, then it tends to attract further growth, accumulating more investment in a self-reinforcing process occurring over indefinite periods of time. The example of Italy is a clear one for Britain. At the time of the unification of the country in the 1860s, the north-western areas around Milan held an initial advantage in terms of early factory development, and in the levels of literacy and political awareness which support economic development. The opening of southern Italian markets to producers in the north greatly increased their sales there and thus put southern craft industry out of business.

The Swedish writer, Myrdal, argued that the play of market forces encouraged urbanisation. Thus the industrialisation of north-western Italy was made the more profitable by the economies of scale described by the term 'agglomeration'. Expansion generated further advance rather than promoting growth in the south. This happened in many different ways. Labour would migrate, in Italy from south to north, and since the migrants tended to be younger and more able workers, the south would be left with a less successful trained workforce. Money would also move from south to north. Any capital generated from profits in the south would be drawn through the national banking system to earn higher profits in northern business. The declining profits of southern business would produce less money in southern taxes and so to the provision of poorer health and education over long periods. These processes would feed into a complex pattern of social 'backwardness', and in this case high birth rates are seen to have delayed the achievement of higher income levels per head.

The concept of cumulative causation does, however, allow for a number of counter-flows or 'spread effects' (although a range of alternative terms exists). The concept of 'spread effects' was based on the view that the growth of a successful region will *eventually* have a stimulating effect on neighbouring regions, through, for instance, the demand for goods or the 'diffusion' (spread) of new technical ideas. However, some writers foresaw that regional imbalance would cause political complaints from the people of poorer areas, and that these would cause the national government to intervene, with measures which *might* eventually be powerful enough to cause 'convergence' toward an 'equilibrium' position.

There is no full agreement as to the truth of these propositions. Myrdal argued that the success of government intervention might be long delayed, and others asserted that governments could only tinker with the underlying forces in question. The main evidence *for* 'convergence' over the longer term comes from 'new' countries such as the USA or Australia. Pioneer areas like the 'Wild West' of US cowboy films eventually caught up on the standard of living of New York. The evidence from Italy, however, where government used almost all the financial incentives imaginable to attract industry to the south, is that four decades of policy have failed to redress its relative backwardness. Evidence of regional inequalities of income is widespread in the European Community states, as shown by Clout (1986). When data are considered carefully, it is difficult in general to find evidence of sustained overall equalisation of income levels between regions. Poor areas do not catch up.

## Cumulative deepening of the north–south divide in the 1950s and 1960s

The familiar long-standing presence of Scots, Irish and Welsh families in the London area is broadly similar to the arrival of workers from the Italian 'periphery' (the south) in the Italian 'core' (the north). The British trend of southward net internal migration dates back to the census of 1921, which was the peak year in the population totals of many mining villages. We have already seen how northern regions suffered a declining *share* of the total British population from 1921 to 1991 (see Fig. 1.3). In the post-war period the total population of these northern regions as a whole did increase, but at a lower rate than in the rest of Britain. The Northern Region, Northern Ireland and Wales tended in those years to have birth rates *above* the national average. In the 15 years between 1951 and 1966, Scotland had the highest percentage natural increase but lost almost equal numbers through net emigration.

Powerful economic factors were reducing the growth of population by pulling people away gradually to regions of relatively greater demand for labour. In turn, the same industries whose national problems created the 'depressed areas' of the 1930s again reduced their demand for labour. The labour force in textiles shrank by 40 per cent from 1951 to 1971, and mining by 53 per cent. Within the coal mining industry, pit closures fell not so much in the Yorkshire and Nottinghamshire coalfields as in the 'peripheral' areas of Scotland and north-east England, where also closures of shipyards and difficulties in the iron and steel industry earned government recognition for the 'regional problem' of these areas by 1963, when this term was officially used for the first time.

It is useful to clarify where the blame lies for these 'regional problems'. The dominant factor is dependence on industries that were declining nationally. It is possible to calculate just what would have happened to the total of jobs in each region if each of their industries had reduced (or increased) its workforce at just the national rate. The 'expected' decline could then be said to be due to 'structural' factors, the relative weight of declining (or expanding) industries in the overall pattern of industries in those areas. Calculations for this period confirm that the 'structural' factor was indeed negative and significant in all regions except the South East and the West Midlands. Those two areas enjoyed a concentration of the growing industries, which in this period were electrical engineering (with a growth of 51 per cent in its workforce, 1951–71) and mechanical engineering (plus 21 per cent). Figure 3.1 shows how the 'expected' rate of change, shown by pecked lines, was in three cases out of four close to the expected outcome. The North West is seen to be suffering very predictable employment decline compared with the South East.

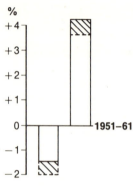

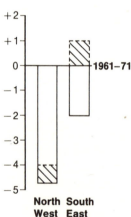

Pecked line represents expected value due to industrial composition of area – the *structural shift*.

Solid bar represents *actual* recorded value.

The difference is known as the *differential shift*.

Fig.3.1 Manufacturing employment change, actual and expected, 1951–71.

*Source:* Law (1980) – see Fig.2.5.

26

Cumulative factors, of the kind discussed earlier, generally added to this structural effect on employment levels. For example, on the one hand it was difficult for redundant workers from large mines or shipyards to set up new small businesses. In the South East and West Midlands, however, the network of small firms provided a healthy seed-bed for further growth from which people developed the skills to start a firm, which enhanced the market advantages which were noted pre-war. The higher incomes in the South East, which contributed to higher standards of housing, education and health, were also accompanied by higher than average levels of government spending, for instance on commuter rail services. The first long-distance motorway, the M1, opened in 1958, was the 'London–Birmingham motorway', and the first long-distance rail electrification (1967) was from London to Birmingham, Manchester and Liverpool. Locational advantages of this belt were thus strengthened, and contributed to factory and office growth. The expansion of the economy created labour shortages which reduced rates of unemployment below the level of 1 per cent over much of the 'axial belt', on average over the whole 20-year period, 1945–65 (Fig. 3.2).

Fig.3.2 Unemployment and factory movement, 1945–65.
(a) Average percentage rates of unemployment over the 20 years 1945–65. Registered wholly unemployed divided by the 'insured population' (employees plus unemployed).

*Source:* Ministry of Labour.

(b) Origins and destinations of factory movement. White circles are proportional in size to the gross number of jobs gained, by 1966, from the movement of factories within the UK 1945–65; black circles to the attributed origins of these moves. These demonstrate movement from areas of low to high unemployment rates.

*Source:* Board of Trade.

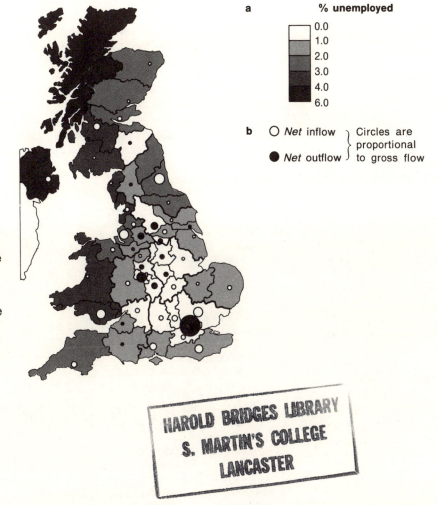

a  % unemployed

0.0
1.0
2.0
3.0
4.0
6.0

b  ○ *Net* inflow ⎫ Circles are proportional
   ● *Net* outflow ⎭ to gross flow

### Answers to the regional problem?

As the first country to enter the Industrial Revolution, Britain suffered some of the worst problems of depression in the inter-war 'downswing', and in 1945 became the first to establish a government regional policy to redress the problems. This response was of the kind anticipated in the analysis above. The traditional view had been that governments should not intervene at all in the decisions of private industry. That was until 1936 when public concern over unemployment prompted the building of the first government industrial estates to encourage the provision of jobs in the depressed areas (Table 3.1). Already by 1940, the report of the Royal Commission on the Distribution of the Industrial Population (the Barlow Report) was recommending a more comprehensive approach to the problem, and wartime circumstances only added to the favourable climate for new laws.

The new policies of 1945 were initiated by a 'coalition' government (that is, one of all the political parties) and used by both Labour and Conservative governments until 1980. While Labour had a natural interest in their own Members of Parliament's seats in coalfield areas, the Conservatives also several times revived regional policy, partly to retain popularity and parliamentary seats in relevant areas, but partly to appear as the legitimate government of 'one nation'. It was the Labour government of 1945–50, however, that initiated remarkably tight controls on industrial firms' location decisions. As part of the process of erecting a new industrial building or factory extension of more than

**Table 3.1  Industrial estates founded by the British government prior to the Second World War, 1939–45**

| Name | Location | Year established | Hectares | Employment by 1955 |
|---|---|---|---|---|
| **Central Scotland Special Area** | | | | |
| Hillington | Near Glasgow | 1937 | 117 | 20,400 |
| Carfin | North Lanarkshire | 1937 | 11 | 930 |
| Chapelhall | North Lanarkshire | 1938 | 14 | 600 |
| Larkhall | North Lanarkshire | 1937 | 14 | 1,600 |
| **South Wales Special Area** | | | | |
| Treforest | Pontypridd | 1936 | 64 | 10,400 |
| **North Eastern Special Area** | | | | |
| Team Valley | Gateshead | 1936 | 267 | 13,100 |
| Pallion | Sunderland | 1938 | 22 | 3,800 |
| West Auckland | Bishop Auckland | 1938 | 11 | 1,900 |
| **West Cumberland Special Area** | | | | |
| Solway | Workington | 1938 | 11 | 1,800 |

*Source:* Industrial Estate Management Corporations.

The Team Valley industrial estate at Gateshead near Newcastle upon Tyne.

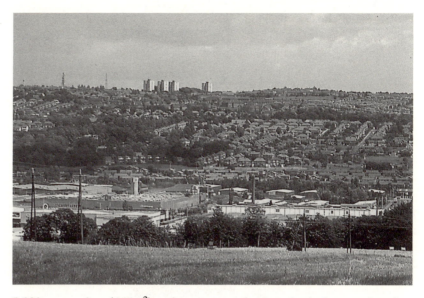

5,000 square feet (465m$^2$), a firm was required to obtain from national government an 'industrial development certificate' stating that the development was 'consistent with the proper distribution of industry'. Especially in congested areas of the south like north-west London, these certificates were frequently refused, with a reminder that the firm might consider placing its new project in one of the government's 'Development Areas'. There is an example in the next chapter of a leading West Midlands firm, Cadbury-Schweppes, setting up branches in Development Areas after the refusal of certificates for their Birmingham site (pages 36–37).

Development Areas were designated problem areas and comprised the 1934 'Special Areas' of Central Scotland, the industrial North East, west Cumbria and the South Wales coalfield, together with new extensions and additions after 1945, notably Merseyside (not so much an 'industrial area' as a declining port). The main attraction of locating in these Areas was subsidised cheap rents on the government's expanding industrial estates. However, the fresh decline of heavy industry prompted a long series of changes in the decade beginning in 1958. Firms setting up in the specified areas could now rely on getting a standard proportion of their building and machinery costs paid by the government. The areas were changed frequently to meet the onset of fresh industrial closures, principally by reference to rates of local unemployment. This measure also brought in seaside resorts and areas like the declining slate-quarrying areas of north Wales.

There were, however, two reactions to this 'blackspots' approach: in 1963 there was an attempt to identify 'growth areas' with the best development *prospects* within otherwise declining regions, but this was largely overtaken by the establishment of broad Development Areas on an almost regional scale from 1965 to 1979. The effects of all these changes were very complicated (not least for the industrialists) and they are summarised in Fig. 3.3, which shows the *number of years* over which individual areas were assisted by regional policy during the period 1934 to 1984. The policy clearly served the whole north and west of Britain but focused most on persistent blackspots.

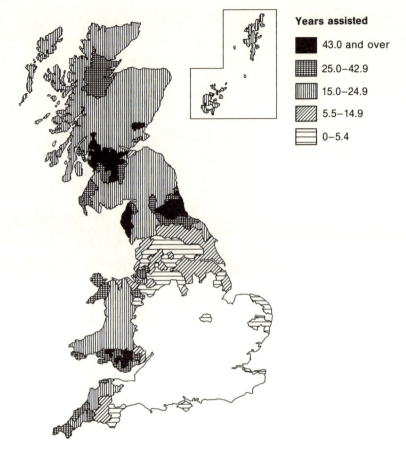

Fig.3.3 'Assisted areas' under regional policy, 1934–84. The map indicates the number of years over which individual areas were classified as Development Areas, Development Districts, Special Development Areas or Intermediate Areas (weighted by status of assistance, which involved more than one level, 1967–84).

*Source:* W.F. Lever (ed.) (1987) *Industrial Change in the UK*, Longman.

**Years assisted**

- 43.0 and over
- 25.0–42.9
- 15.0–24.9
- 5.5–14.9
- 0–5.4

## An evaluation of change

Helped by these policies, many firms established branches in the Development Areas, notably in the expanding industries of electrical engineering and motor vehicles. The Areas dominated the longer-distance movement of industry from the south and from abroad, chiefly the USA. So strongly was this the case that Table 2.1 identified 'national dispersal' as the dominant location trend of the period 1945–75. However, far from being an aberration in industrial location, there is every reason to regard these moves as part of a logical national process of 'deglomeration', or of decentralisation from areas of labour and land shortage in Greater London and the West Midlands to those of crucial labour reserves. This was a movement which policy only reinforced. Many surveys agree that three-quarters of mobile firms regarded labour availability as their prime location factor. However, access to markets remained a consideration, and a firm which was forced, say, to leave Birmingham, would prefer to locate in the Development Areas of South Wales or Merseyside than in more distant ones in Scotland, to minimise separation from established markets.

The principal destinations of long-distance factory movement between 1945 and 1965 are shown in Fig. 3.2 by open circles, proportionate in size to the number of jobs established in the resulting branch factories by 1966. These were mainly in areas of higher unemployment, attracted there by labour availability, and are matched by black circles in the areas of 'origin', proportionate in size to the number of jobs transferred by outward movement; these are mainly in areas of low unemployment. All in all, the number of jobs moved between regions from 1945 to 1965 amounted to 422,000, or 8 per cent of the total number of factory jobs in the country as a whole. In the period from 1965 to 1975, a further 130,000 jobs were moved, on similar definitions. On wider measures of the success of regional policy there is less agreement. A government estimate of 1979 was that regional policy had by then directly created between 250,000 and 445,000 additional jobs. The numbers would be increased to the range between 350,000 and 650,000 if wider effects were taken into account, including a second round of jobs created through the spending of employers and employees in the new areas.

However, this was 'like trying to walk up a down escalator', as mining and older manufacturing continued to decline in the peripheral coalfields. Data for *total* employment of all kinds across the regions of Britain (Fig. 3.4) show that their relative fate was little altered. A substantial national increase of employment of 6.5 per cent included widespread gains in the number of jobs in the West Midlands (a gain of 9.8 per cent) and in the South East (12.2 per cent), with even larger rates of increase in adjoining regions. There were very small gains in the number of jobs in the Northern Region and Wales, and small reductions in remaining regions of the north. A year-by-year study of all the northern regions taken together, from 1947 to 1988, shows only three years in which their gain or loss of jobs was more favourable than in the southern regions, also taken together. These were the years 1973 to 1975, when the accumulated effect of ten years of 'strengthened' regional policy was just enough to tip the overall balance of change in favour of the assisted regions.

Fig.3.4 Changes in regional employment and population, 1951–71.

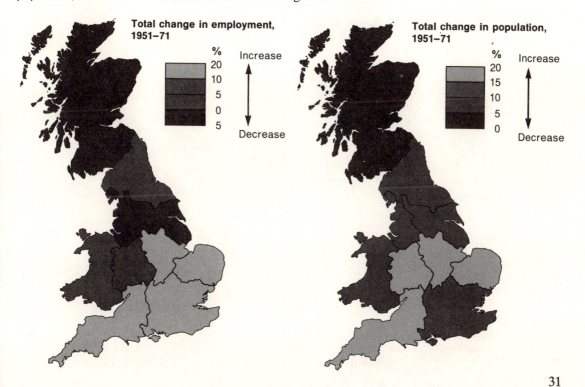

## The 'drift to the south'

Not surprisingly, the record revealed by the 1951 and 1971 censuses of population (Fig. 3.4) is similar to the employment trends. The South East gained 1.9 million of the total population increase of 4.9 million, although its rate of growth, 12.6 per cent, was exceeded by all the adjoining regions and the West Midlands. Most regions to the north did show a gain of total population, but this was despite a net loss of people through migration in every case. What becomes clear through looking more closely at the figures is that this movement to the south failed to satisfy the area's need for workers. It is here that we find the reason for strong Commonwealth immigration to Britain in this period: immigrant labour was needed. Figure 3.5 demonstrates the location in Britain of increases in numbers of overseas-born citizens between the 1961 and 1966 censuses. They avoided the 'peripheral areas', with their less buoyant labour market, and settled particularly in London, Birmingham and textile-producing areas such as Bradford and Leicester, where their work was much in demand. Many of the London immigrants worked in low-paid jobs in transport and hospitals, because the British-born workforce had a wide choice of more congenial and relatively well-paid jobs in expanding sectors.

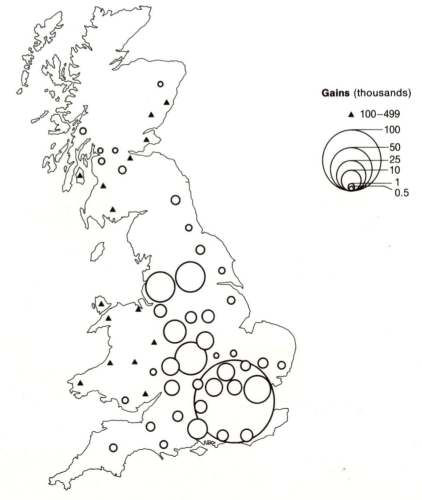

Fig.3.5 Changes in the location of overseas-born people, 1961–66.

*Source:* Coates, B.E. and Rawstron, E.M. (1971) *Regional Variations in Britain: studies in economic and social geography*, Batsford, London.

32

The bleak urban landscape of central London in the 1960s.

It was becoming clear that the key growth sector in London was that of office employment. Of course, London's international and national role in government and finance had sustained its growing population during the industrialisation of other regions. Now this turned into a stronger *structural* advantage over other regions, as service employment growth accelerated in the first half of the 1960s. The fitting of new offices into the London map and its skyline became a big problem, as did the accommodation of increased numbers of rail commuters on what is now Network Southeast.

Government therefore attempted to move offices out of London in much the same way as it had moved manufacturing. In general, it proved difficult to relocate offices very far, although the government was more successful in moving its own civil service work to cities such as Liverpool and Glasgow. Private offices were able to move, however, as far as the New Towns of Milton Keynes and Northampton, which were planned in the government's South East Study of 1964.

In retrospect it can be argued that the inability of regional policy to incorporate office and white-collar activity in long-distance movement was its downfall. In the new 'downswing' after the mid-1960s the policy was relying on a sector of the economy – manufacturing – which was no longer expanding its overall need for workers. However, with average transport costs in manufacturing much lower – only 5.6 per cent of the value of factory output by 1963 – movement within Britain had certainly proved feasible in a wide range of activities. In many ways, government policy had been running with the grain of events in encouraging firms to relocate in order to find labour. The issue, however, is whether it could have done more, or indeed was intending to do more, than counter a little the general 'drift to the south', to the area with all the structural and locational advantages. We have seen that the policy reversed the drift in a few years of the early 1970s. After that date, in fact, the European Commission reports that income differences between regions increased in several European countries. The evidence supports the view of many theorists that the process of moderating regional differences is at best slow and beset by many difficulties. However, net outward migration from northern Britain would have created even more problems for people in both north and south if it had not been for regional policy.

The DHSS moved out in the 1960s to Longbenton, near Newcastle upon Tyne.

# 4 The role of individual companies in post-war patterns

As the limited effect of regional measures came to be realised, so other aspects of location and change were emphasised. It was appreciated that the form of ownership of factories was important. A different decision could result from a large industrial enterprise with many plants – a 'multi-plant' firm – than from a local independent firm in a similar situation. In both cases, decision-makers could act without full knowledge of the relevant facts and with personal objectives of their own. This chapter is concerned with individual companies and the relationships between them. It refers both to large companies, like Imperial Chemical Industries (ICI), and to small firms.

## The fall and rise of small firms

A firm is simply a commercial enterprise under the law. Small firms will be considered before multi-plant organisations. It may seem surprising that the *revival* of small firms is an important feature today in Britain and Europe. It must be asked whether they can make a significant contribution to regional economic development or reduce the north–south divide. From 1935 to the 1960s, the number of small enterprises in British manufacturing was halved from about 136,000 to 66,000. It then climbed back to 87,000 in the early 1980s, and had increased by at least another quarter by 1990.

In locational terms the revival of small firms contributed, from the 1970s, to a dominant trend towards decentralisation from urban to rural areas, though not from south to north. Detailed work by geographers demonstrated many more location factors at work among the general mass of firms than just the attraction of financial inducements or labour supply in Development Areas. Although the effects of international and national economic competition were important, these must be considered in conjunction with the background, motives, knowledge and incentives of the owners of firms. Faced with barriers to expansion at an existing factory, some unambitious owners might feel satisfied with keeping their business at its existing size, while others would think of different forms of expansion and receive information about alternative sites in different ways. Some might be swayed by reports about the possible quality of staff in particular areas, and others by the likely way of life for their own families if they moved.

The same kind of locational research among the large numbers of plants traditionally found in cities also revealed new complexity. Locational and employment *adjustments* were found to be going on all the time, with the opening, closure, expansion and contraction of factories and workshops. Differences in the overall employment trends of, say, Manchester and Glasgow, might turn on quite a narrow difference between the numbers of factory openings and closures. The general trend, however, was one of factory employment decline in the cities. Inner London experienced a net decline of factory jobs as early as the 1956–61 period, and this was general to inner cities by the years 1965–75.

### Industrial linkage in cities

One objection that was traditionally raised to the policies of moving firms from a large manufacturing city like Birmingham, say, to Development Areas or New Towns was that local businesses all depended on each other and could not be geographically separated. Firms were thought to benefit from trading with each other, as, for instance, in the Birmingham metal trades. In other words, they experienced 'agglomeration economies'. The efficiency and viability of all the firms were thought to benefit from proximity between plants, and the term 'industrial linkage' was applied to such patterns of local trade in supplies and products between manufacturing plants.

Studies of London and Birmingham showed that by the 1970s industrial linkage, in the strict sense of trade in physical goods, had in fact declined, though certain industries in both cities still found half of their supplies and markets locally. In Birmingham the firms concerned were small, privately owned and backward. In London, linkage was found in trades with a market concentrated in a particular part of the city. In both cases it appeared that the value of firms' proximity to each other lay not so much in bulk exchanges as in dependence on each other for urgent assistance or for exchanging information, for instance in fashion goods.

If linkage, which had been thought so important in sustaining London and the industrial conurbations, had declined, perhaps firms could now move away. In fact the firms that could move out of London were those with least linkages there, while those which had to stay had the closest dependence on other firms there. But linkages were not a heavy restriction. Generally firms increasingly rejected the advantages of geographical proximity to other firms and industries.

The freedom to move, in the case of London to all the surrounding counties, has already been shown (see Fig. 3.2). This form of decentralisation from cities was of sufficient importance as a location trend to qualify as a separate entry, 'regional dispersal' (row 7) in Table 2.1. It was sufficient to add strongly to the growth of East Anglia. Research in that region confirmed that, while firms moving into the area could usefully form new linkages there, they were by no means essential, because those in London, for example, could easily be stretched over a greater distance.

The significance of this research was to show that decentralisation of small and medium-sized firms from cities was possible, but on an intra-regional scale, rather than on a long-distance scale which could benefit the Development Areas. As London was the major source of the flow it tended to benefit many of the other southern counties. These more rural areas in turn proved more fertile than northern industrial areas in generating the birth and survival of local (indigenous) small firms (see also Chapter 8).

### The significance of 'multi-plant enterprises'

There are about 4,000 private-sector manufacturing enterprises in the UK operating more than one plant, and they account for nearly three-quarters of total employment in manufacturing. Among these, in 1988, the largest 100 enterprises were running 3,086 businesses with 1.5 million workers, or 30 per cent of the total in manufacturing. Measured in financial terms these were led by ICI (Imperial Chemical Industries), Unilever (in food and fats) and the General Electric Company. Not all establishments run under their parents' names.

The significance of these large enterprises can hardly be underestimated. They were described in the 1970s as the 'meso-economy', capable together of dominating the national economy, and of challenging government's regional development policies by threatening to move their investments abroad, as did the US computer firm, IBM. The numbers of multi-plant enterprises in leading industries had increased rapidly in the 1960s both through the establishment of new branches, and by the acquisition of existing firms across all the regions. A local plant has now to be seen in the context of the parent enterprise as a whole and its divisions. The central organisation, working impersonally from a distance, can allot a particular specialised role to the plant within its overall chain of production, and choose whether to expand this or another plant. Generally, when firms are taken over, their managerial and white-collar work is moved to the headquarters area, which for British corporations is characteristically in London or the South East.

The benefits of multi-plant enterprises, including over 1,000 foreign firms running factories in Britain, can be hotly debated. On the one hand, local factors of agglomeration are less important to them and they can move over greater distances in establishing or acquiring branches. They bring greater resources of finance, technology, marketing and administration to acquired firms. On the other hand, it is now possible to find whole regions where three-quarters of manufacturing activity is run by enterprises with headquarters elsewhere. Over half the foreign activity in the UK is controlled from the USA. This 'external control' is much criticised, above all for the possible uncertainties which it may bring in continuity of work. On the other hand, most regions will today readily welcome, for example, a new Japanese factory. To understand the evolution of multi-plant location patterns we will study the examples of two leading enterprises.

### Cadbury-Schweppes plc

This large enterprise, which makes chocolate, other confectionery, and soft drinks both in Britain and abroad, resulted from the merging of two companies. The map of their factories reflects many of the features of a multi-plant firm (Fig. 4.1). The principal factory is an early example of suburban decentralisation, from the city of Birmingham to the new suburb Bournville, which the Cadbury family created in 1879. The second most important – Fry's at Somerdale near Bristol – was acquired in the 1920s. In the post-war period Cadbury's established three branches in Development Areas: one on Merseyside was initiated

Fig.4.1 Cadbury-
Schweppes plc.
Factories are shown by
the number of
employees, end 1991.

*Source:* Cadbury-Schweppes.

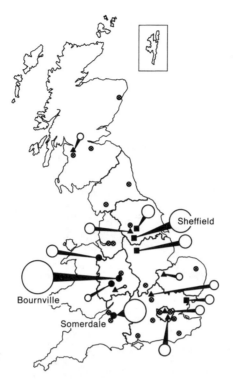

● Cadbury Ltd
■ Trebor Bassett Ltd
▲ Soft drinks factories
⊗ Depots

Sheffield

Bournville

Somerdale

**Total employees**

3,000
1,000
500

Cadbury's principal
factory is at Bournville,
near Birmingham.

through the refusal of an industrial development certificate at
Bournville (this was sold with other plants in 1988); one (now closed) at
Catterick in North Yorkshire was reckoned as the most profitable site to
process potatoes in their production areas; and one (still open) at Chirk,
just west of the Welsh border, was established to process cocoa beans
from Liverpool for onward distribution. In the late 1980s the firm sold
some miscellaneous food factories and bought Trebor Bassett Ltd,
mainly in Yorkshire. The bottling and distribution of soft drinks by
Schweppes was altogether a much more market-oriented activity, which
involved 7 factories and 29 depots, serving subregional markets, as
recently as 1984. However, as in other drinks industries, many smaller
units have been closed to be replaced by large automatic plants,
including the firm's new development, Europe's largest soft drinks
factory, near the M1 and M62 at Wakefield.

*Imperial Chemical Industries (ICI)*

Britain's biggest manufacturing business, ICI, has a location pattern
that is traditionally centred in the north on raw materials (Fig. 4.2).
However, it developed in a later phase of national expansion than many
heavy industries, as a result of the merger in 1926 of three companies
which had already, in turn, acquired smaller ones. ICI Fertilisers, at
Billingham (Cleveland), was based on deposits of underground salt and
supply trains of Durham coal. ICI General Chemicals grew up on the
basis of Cheshire salt supplies at Runcorn. The Nobel Explosives
Company utilised isolated sand dunes to provide protection in making
its product at Stevenston (Strathclyde), and ICI Colours and Fine
Chemicals (Blackley, Manchester) owed its location to linkage with the
north-west textiles market.

ICI works at Billingham,
Teesside.

37

Fig.4.2 Imperial Chemical
Industries (ICI). Factory
groups are shown by
number of employees,
end 1990.

*Source:* ICI.

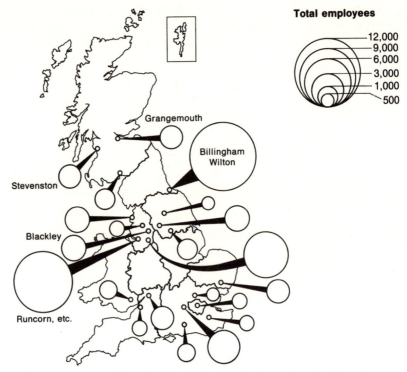

**Total employees**

12,000
9,000
6,000
3,000
1,000
500

Grangemouth

Billingham
Wilton

Stevenston

Blackley

Runcorn, etc.

Inter-war expansion occurred principally through extensions to
existing plants, because internal economies of scale were large.
However, post-war expansion was so great as to justify development of
the large new complex of Wilton Works (Cleveland), which increasingly
used oil imports via the River Tees; it is run by the Petrochemicals
Division. Development Area status was a supporting factor in this
decision, and accelerated the growth of several ICI plants in other areas
in the 1960s and 1970s. In one case in 1958 the special financial
inducements of the Northern Ireland government prompted ICI Fibres
to establish a factory there, at Kilroot, rather than at Hull, but it closed
in 1981. Indeed, since that date ICI has been forced to run down its
fertiliser and bulk chemicals output in favour of lighter products which
were previously only sidelines. These provide more stable work most
significantly at five locations in the South East outside London, but also
in Cheshire.

### 'Growth centres' in regional development

These two case studies show that in the long term the spatial growth of
multi-plant enterprises tends to produce increasingly dispersed patterns
of manufacturing activity across the national map. The enterprises
separately accumulate plants which were established in different past
'layers' of industrial investment, in Victorian cities, in areas of raw
materials, on market-oriented sites and, in the earlier post-war period,
in places with available labour. In view of this complex pattern it is
debated whether the advantages of nineteenth-century agglomeration
can be created again. Can local linkage of the plants of *different*
enterprises, large and small, help to create self-sustaining growth in the

development of regions, as it did in Victorian cities? Can regional policy do more than attract enterprises *separately* to establish plants in Development Areas? These questions have persisted since the 1960s and 1970s, when the later phases of the long 'post-war boom' were still generating heavy industrial investment in Britain and Europe.

International theory and practice in the 1960s took the view that central planning by governments could foster 'growth centres' at chosen points on the map. To counter the tendency for national growth to centralise in favoured regions of a country, it was proposed that the pull of established centres could be countered by a spatial strategy of development elsewhere. This was more than a matter of defining 'assisted areas' on the map, and it was the opposite of identifying 'blackspots'. The aim was to concentrate many inter-related kinds of investment at a favoured growth centre within a generally deprived area. Much would be gained from concentrating public investment at growth centres in infrastructure – in transport, housing, electricity, etc. This would help to attract industry, not only to share these common facilities ('economies of urbanisation') but also to enjoy the advantages of trading between each other (industrial linkage or 'economies of localisation').

The concept of industrial linkage tended at that time to focus on large plants. For example, an oil refinery might be followed by the building of a petrochemicals works to take part of its refined oil as a feedstock (a raw material) for processing into many kinds of specialised chemicals. This would be an example of 'downstream' linkage, because manufacturing would be taking place at a later stage in the flow of the raw material, oil, from the ground to the state of a finished product (such as nylon) than in the refinery itself. An example of 'upstream' linkage would be the attraction of firms to the same region to make the machinery used in a refinery or processing plant.

The growth-centre concept was taken further, for instance in European Community recommendations for southern Italy, and detailed plans were made to build up a sequence of new plants to complement and support each other through linkage in a single complex. This was similar to the 'maritime production complex' of west European geographers. In the 1960s and 1970s, two heavy industries, steel and oil-refining, were increasingly utilising larger bulk shipments of imported iron ore and crude oil at large new plants, which were deliberately situated on deep maritime estuaries so as to eliminate transport costs between ship and works. As refinery gases are difficult and costly to transport over long distances, petrochemicals works based on this source are located adjacent to the refinery (and they also feed back materials to it). Developments on the European seaboard, for instance at Fos-sur-Mer in southern France, or on the Setubal peninsula, Portugal, were thus described as 'maritime industrial complexes'. In the UK, the concept of growth centres was used to support regional policy only temporarily, from 1963 to 1965. As we shall see, industrial components were traded over much longer distances in Britain. However, areas such as Teesside appeared to develop independently as 'maritime industrial complexes'.

### Linked complexes in Britain? The example of Teesside, Cleveland

In Britain, petrochemicals certainly developed in order to tap adjacent oil refineries, for example at Fawley on Southampton Water, and at Baglan Bay near Swansea; the full range of examples is shown in Fig. 4.3. Well over half the production of refined oil was in northern regions of Britain, because there were more suitable ports there. It is of particular interest to study the example of ICI Petrochemicals, Wilton Works, Cleveland (Fig. 4.4). From 1965 this was increasingly fed, via a pipeline under the Tees, by the ICI/Phillips oil refinery. In a continuous period of plant building, different divisions, together employing up to 15,000 people, were sited at Wilton to make use of its petrochemical feedstocks and common services in making products such as nylon, perspex and terylene. Clearly the possibilities for linkages *between* plants and divisions, which were served by 59 kilometres of internal roads, were immense, and were augmented by pipeline and other linkages with ICI Billingham, and indeed with ICI works in other regions.

Linkage *within* an individual enterprise does not, however, constitute the linkage *between* enterprises and industries that was sought by the 'growth-centre' theory. Only 5 per cent of tonnage deliveries by ICI Wilton were made within Cleveland (and only 4 per cent in the rest of the Northern Region). Its main customers lay elsewhere; even new

Fig.4.3 Principal oilfields, oil refineries and petrochemicals works in Britain.

*Sources:* Ordnance Survey and Country Life Publications (1982).

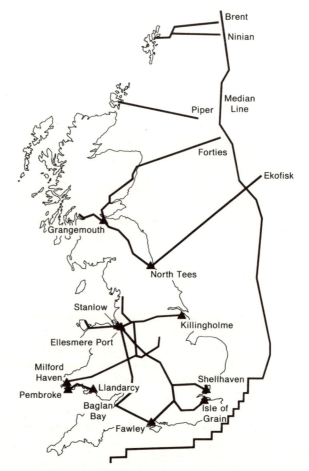

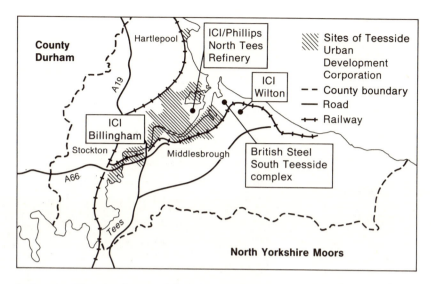

Fig.4.4 The county of Cleveland in north-east England, including ICI and British Steel.

industries like plastics moulding found it more profitable to receive bulk supplies from Wilton in market-oriented locations such as the South East, than to move to Cleveland. Only a handful of firms ever did so, and these were financially related to ICI.

The position can be corroborated both by the steel industry in Cleveland (Fig. 4.4) and by petrochemicals elsewhere. In the past, Cleveland's steel industry had spawned several large 'downstream' consumers of local steel in the establishment of heavy engineering works and shipbuilding yards. However, these had tended to close and not be replaced, so that by the 1960s the leading steel-making firm sold only 16 per cent of its product in Cleveland, though all these steel-making firms delivered 25–30 per cent within the Northern Region. The British Steel Corporation's 'South Teesside Complex' today has many internal linkages achieved by internal railways, but it is increasingly engaged in making a specialised product – structural steel – for the *national market*.

In the 1960s, observers were struck by the apparent number of firms in Scotland's Grangemouth petrochemicals complex on the Firth of Forth. However, many of the firms there are jointly owned by the refinery proprietors, BP; so we cannot say that individual independent firms have been heavily attracted there. In turn, studies of oil and petrochemicals abroad, for example at Europoort, Netherlands, and in the former Soviet Union, suggest that, whatever may happen within the enterprise, heavy industry, so far at least, has mainly developed separately rather than through the linkages promised by 'growth centres'. The UK position is basically similar: apparent 'growth centres' are not benefiting greatly from industrial linkage, but rather from external economies such as the use of common transport facilities.

## Motor industry dispersal and its effects

The motor industry has often captured attention in regional development because of the scale and potential effects of its activities. In international theory it has been seen as a candidate to site 'downstream' of an iron and steel works. There are few examples of this happening, and none in Britain. However, it was the leading sector in the 1960s movement of industry in Britain, and there were high hopes that motor components suppliers would move to 'downstream' locations near new vehicle factories in order to win supply contracts. There had been few important motor vehicle makers in Britain's assisted areas up to the 1960s. In that period government firmly used the 'stick and carrot' of regional policy, industrial development certificates and financial inducements. That succeeded in relocating expansions, for example of Ford from Dagenham (Greater London) to Halewood (Merseyside) and Swansea (West Glamorgan), and Vauxhall from Luton (Bedfordshire) to Ellesmere Port (Cheshire); see Fig. 4.5.

The Ford Motor Company at Halewood, Merseyside, covers a wide area and employs thousands of people.

o Ford

▲ Vauxhall

■ Rootes Group

● Triumph

♦ BMC

* Now closed

Fig.4.5 The dispersal of vehicle industry expansions of the 1960s from the South East and West Midlands to Wales, the North West (Merseyside) and Scotland.

It was confidently expected that many of their suppliers would relocate with the assembly plants and that they would also generate an element of spontaneous self-sustaining growth in engineering and other trades in Central Scotland and Merseyside. Nearly three decades later, however, the evidence is indisputable. Only a small number of factories were established to supply the new motor factories. Geographers concluded that Central Scotland was too small for a growth-centre policy to have much effect on faster growth designed to gain economies of urbanisation or localisation. Scottish and Merseyside plants were supplied from the West Midlands and the south. Three have now closed, those at Linwood, Bathgate and Speke. Much later, in the 1980s, more evidence has emerged from the location of the Japanese plant Nissan in north-east England (and of Japanese plants in the USA). Motor car plants are supplied from fairly wide areas, certainly wider than an English region, partly because no individual component maker wishes to rely on contracts with just one customer, and similarly car makers do not want to rely on just one component supplier.

## The 'spatial division of labour'

It is too soon to dismiss all 'growth-centre' policies: they may work in different countries over a longer period of time. However, to concentrate solely on this aspect of regional development is to miss the fundamental change wrought by the dominance of multi-plant enterprises and the reasons why they may invest in new locations. As they can take advantage of declining transport costs to move goods between their plants on a national and international scale, they normally have relatively few interests in the local trading environment of a new factory. In the great majority of long-distance moves since the war, the most attractive factor in 'national dispersal' (Table 2.1, row 8) was that of available labour.

A further disappointment to the receiving regions, however, has been that these firms' demands for labour have been biased towards lower grades of work, towards the semi-skilled occupations of assembly, routine machine operation, or sewing. Thus the difference between, say, the West Midlands and Strathclyde is no longer that the one concentrated on the lighter metal trades and the other on engineering and shipbuilding, but that the former now concentrates on traditional skilled trades, and the latter on semi-skilled work in British or American branch factories. Massey (1979) observed that whereas in the nineteenth century different regions tended to specialise in different *industrial* sectors such as shipbuilding, the specialisation in the late twentieth century is by *occupation*, such as assembly or administration.

The significance of this change for regional development is to illuminate the poorer *quality* of the available replacement jobs in peripheral areas. With a bias towards lower-paid female work and a relative absence of white-collar and decision-making jobs, the branch factory in northern 'assisted areas' was providing *below average* income, training and economic stimulus to its receiving area. These mass-production factories were altogether different from the traditional skilled factories of Birmingham and the traditional manufacturing town.

In contrast, however, we can note how ICI employ greater proportions of research and development staff in the counties around London. Multi-plant corporations have increasingly separated these types of occupation, e.g. semi-skilled, skilled, research, clerical and administrative, between different sites. They have utilised different regions in different ways.

It is this which Massey dubbed the 'spatial division of labour', as recognised in Table 2.1. In turn, however, many geographers now think of the 'new international division of labour', under which enterprises locate new semi-skilled factories, and increasingly some skilled activities, in countries of the economically developing world, for purposes of recruiting cheap labour.

## The rise of new 'industrial districts'

We found in this chapter that industrial enterprises had increasingly been going their own way in choosing locations for investment. This applies to both large and small enterprises, although the capacity of movement in smaller firms is regularly limited by distance. Industrial movement and change are occurring all the time and the established pattern results from superimposition of all the past layers of Table 2.1 on top of each other. The next chapter will show that it was the closure of factories that was the dominant feature of the 1980s, and consequently there was little incentive to move to the 'assisted areas' for labour.

If, however, we were to add a new row to Table 2.1 it might refer to 'flexible production' and 'vertical disintegration', implying that decisions of the late 1980s and the 1990s had reversed several of our conclusions in this chapter. Large enterprises had previously been amassing more facilities, believing that it was cheaper to undertake different tasks themselves – that is, vertical integration. Now it is widely held among international geographers that many large enterprises have found it cheaper to have some of those tasks, for instance making components, done by separate firms. It is even thought that some of these firms which undertake subcontracts for bigger plants may need to locate in the same area as those plants. Thus, after a period of discrediting industrial linkage, geographers claim to have rediscovered it in new 'industrial districts'. They certainly exist in some countries, but there is no agreement yet on their existence in Britain.

# 5 De-industrialisation and the 'north–south divide'

So far, this book has assumed that industry was a source of growth, in fact the main source of growth, in regional change. In each 'long wave' over the period since the Industrial Revolution, some industries went into decline. The 'downswing' which was centred on the 1930s confirmed the relative decline of the 'peripheral' coalfield regions. But even there, industrial recovery, replacement and war demand eventually provided factory jobs, and these coalfield areas later received some new factories under regional policy. The other industrial regions, which were more important in size of population and output, continued as diverse, fully employed economies by replacing those firms which did fall into decline. As we noticed, the 'axial belt' of industry, including the country's manufacturing heartland – the West Midlands, the East Midlands, Yorkshire and Humberside and the North West – showed very low unemployment figures at least until the 1960s.

The essential point about the 1970s and 1980s was that a fresh 'downswing' in the long cycle extended the problems of the 'peripheral' coalfield regions to most of this heartland. Thus the West Midlands, Yorkshire and Humberside and the North West (but not the East Midlands) were added to Scotland, Wales and the Northern Region to form a much wider area of difficulty, now identified as a whole as the 'north' of the 'north–south divide'. By 1980, industrial closures and job losses had spread to all the cities and industrial areas of the north. The 'assisted areas' of regional policy were changed by 1984 to include, for example, Birmingham and Manchester; but the policy now had even less success, and previous Development Area factories closed, including some of those of ICI, Cadbury-Schweppes and the car industry. Unemployed workers were unable to get jobs because so many kinds of industry, of all ages, had reduced their needs for workers. Many large industrial towns which had never before met serious difficulties now had high unemployment, with reductions in the income, living standards and health of many families. It appeared, therefore, that for a town to enter this period with a high dependence on industrial jobs from the past had become a severe disadvantage.

## De-industrialisation

This process of change was so general that it is described by the term 'de-industrialisation'. Its origins are seen by many in terms of the country's inability to 'pay its way' in the world. By 1982, for the first time since the Industrial Revolution, the country's exports of manufactured goods fell below the value of manufactured imports. This financial loss was made up by some improvement in other sectors. Britain continued to pay less to primary producing countries for food and raw materials. But its balance of payments was sustained by trade in fuel, arising chiefly from the high production levels of North Sea oil and gas (see Fig. 4.3), which reached their peak in the 1980s. These provided a large financial cushion for the country temporarily, until 1988.

With the benefit of hindsight, many people now find the beginnings of Britain's relative world decline early in the cycle of the 1880s to 1930s, in the country's lack of adaptation to changing competitive conditions in industry. Various factors are blamed, including poor education and training, the limited ability of managers and the power of trades unions. However, the country also needed by the 1970s to improve its levels of output per factory worker. Britain was therefore worse placed than other countries to meet international trade competition, and in the years up to 1981 experienced greater proportions of factory job losses and closures than other industrialised countries. In addition, the need persisted to increase output per worker in the years of recovery from 1981 to 1989. This produced continuing job losses. Even when output increased rapidly, this growth of productivity prevented any significant rise in the number of industrial workers.

'De-industrialisation' may therefore be defined not only in terms of a declining ability to compete, but also in the declining number of industrial jobs. The overall number of factory jobs in the economy is shown in Fig. 5.1 (for employment in the coal and energy industries, see Fig. 5.2). After falling gradually through a number of cycles from its peak of 8.5 million in 1966, the number then fell rapidly in a deep recession (1980–81) and continued to decline, though at a reduced rate, during much of the 1980s. It was correct for the government to report an increase of output in this period. By 1988–90 output had at last exceeded its peak of 1974, but employment was much lower, and it is employment that counts in understanding why people work and live where they do.

For the geographer the key point is whether this massive change affected all parts of the country equally. The next section analyses the changes in the number of industrial employees for the period 1971 to 1991 as a whole, which was then the most crucial factor affecting regional change. If, as in 1921–31 (Fig. 2.5) or 1951–71 (Fig. 3.4), job losses were unevenly distributed between industries, then it would be expected that industrial job losses were unevenly spread between regions. If, however, de-industrialisation was more general than in previous 'downswings', then all the regions would suffer in more equal degree.

Fig.5.1 Total employees in the manufacturing industry of Great Britain, 1959–91.

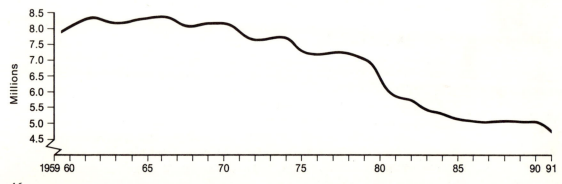

46

### Industrial trends, 1971–91

Writing at the beginning of the 1970s one would have said that industrial decline was concentrated again in particular industries – the same sectors as in the 1930s: coal, iron and steel, shipbuilding and textiles. The electrical engineering industry, including electronics and computer equipment, was recruiting and expanding, and the closure of a large foreign-owned plant was still almost unheard of. During the 1970s, the greatest sources of all job losses lay in the manufacture of textiles, mechanical engineering, and iron and steel. However, from the mid-decade, increasing problems were becoming evident in a wider range of industries, including motor vehicles, and by 1980 severe reductions in industrial jobs became common to virtually all products and manufacturing areas.

Demolition in 1980 of the British Steel factory at Irlam near Manchester.

In the 1980s most industries continued to lose jobs, some in a most persistent manner. The largest reductions in employment occurred in iron and steel, shipbuilding, and motor vehicles. It was only in small, narrowly defined parts of industry that any net increase could be found, for instance in making certain builders' goods. Some electronics consumer goods showed an increase of jobs, but as a whole even electronics and high-technology industries also contributed to employment decline.

On taking the 20-year period 1971–91, it can be seen that industry lost two jobs in every five. This occurred through a great variety of processes, ranging from massive closures involving large-scale redundancies to almost imperceptible change, through firms simply not replacing workers when they left. When we divide industry into four main sectors (Table 5.1), we can see that there was little variation in the percentage rate of decline. The heavy industry sectors of metal manufacturing and chemicals did even worse than coal and energy. There was *relatively* less job loss in 'other manufacturing', which includes textiles, food, timber and paper.

**Table 5.1    Employment decline in industry, by leading sectors, in Great Britain 1971–91**

|  | Employees (thousands) | | Change, 1971–91 | |
|---|---|---|---|---|
|  | 1971 | 1991 | Numbers | % |
| 1  Coal and energy | 790 | 437 | −353 | −44.7 |
| 2  Heavy manufacturing | 1,266 | 682 | −584 | −46.1 |
| 3  Metal-using industries | 3,659 | 2,138 | −1,521 | −41.6 |
| 4  Other manufacturing | 2,987 | 1,939 | −1,048 | −35.1 |
| Total 1–4 | 8,702 | 5,196 | −3,506 | −40.3 |
| Subtotal, manufacturing 2–4 | 7,912 | 4,759 | −3,153 | −39.9 |

*Source:* Official figures via NOMIS; excludes agriculture and services.

Fig.5.2 Employment change in industry, 1971–91. (The four sectors shown here add up to make the total which is shown in Fig.5.3.)

*Source:* NOMIS.

## Regional trends, 1971–91

It is also important to consider whether all major sectors showed even rates of decline across the country. It is possible to study the percentage rate of change of each industry across ten of the eleven regions which we identified in Chapter 1, in the four maps which together make up Fig. 5.2. In 'coal and energy' the number of jobs fell by more than half

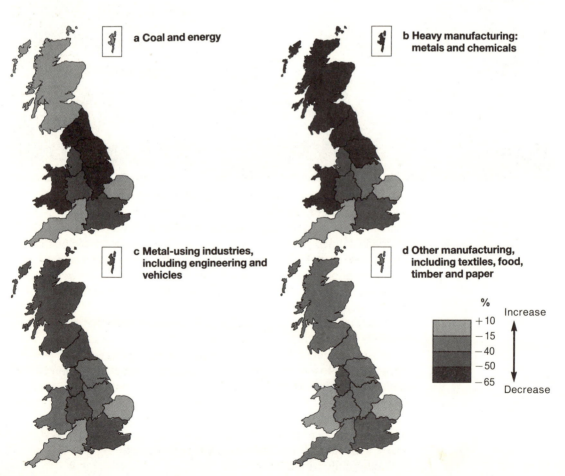

(Fig. 5.2a). In the 1970s, much of this loss was concentrated in Wales (chiefly in the South Wales coalfield) and in the Northern Region of England (chiefly in the Northumberland and Durham coalfield). At the same time new collieries were planned in North Yorkshire, in the Selby coalfield, and in the East Midlands, in Leicestershire. However, after the miners' strike of 1984–85, closures began to occur even in the most successful mining areas of the East Midlands, as the electricity industry prepared to take a greater proportion of its coal needs from abroad. All these trends affected Scotland too, but as the main base from which to exploit North Sea oil, its statistics for coal and energy were offset by new oil jobs principally in and around Aberdeen; hence Scotland stands out on the map from the other coalfield regions.

Confrontation between miners and police during the 1984–85 miners' strike.

In 'heavy manufacturing' (Fig. 5.2b), there was a decline of more than 50 per cent in employment in four regions in which it was traditionally concentrated: Scotland, Wales, the Northern Region and Yorkshire and Humberside. In the iron and steel industry, plans for large increases in production at modern new plant, as installed at Redcar Works in the South Teesside Complex, Cleveland (see Fig. 4.4), were overtaken by big reductions in the demand for steel, accompanied by even bigger reductions in the workforce. Major plants such as Shotton in North Wales, and Consett in the Northern Region, were closed in the early 1980s, but the decade also saw massive reductions in the activity of steel processing centres such as Sheffield. De-industrialisation also occurred in oil and chemicals. Some oil refineries shut, and every division of ICI was forced to make cuts in its staff (see below).

So far, the picture has been of a familiar kind, of heavier industries showing greater proportionate difficulties in northern regions than their representatives in the south. However, Table 5.1 shows that the two sectors which we have considered so far account for little more than a quarter of total industrial job losses. The 'metal-using industries' include the making of an extremely wide range of machines and electrical goods, including motor vehicles, ships and aircraft. Taking them all together, it is remarkable that it is the growth areas of the post-war period (Fig. 5.2c) which show the very biggest reductions: the West Midlands −48.6 per cent, the South East −47.0 per cent. The regions which show the smaller reductions, such as East Anglia −12.3 per cent, and Wales −16.9 per cent, had not been well-established centres of these industries in the past; they have tended therefore to have only the newer sections of them, which have not had so much time to mature and to decline.

Regional employment trends are similar in the remaining parts of manufacturing (as shown in Fig. 5.2d), which include textiles, food, timber and paper. Again, it is the areas where these sectors are long-established which show the greatest rates of decline – the North West −48.6 per cent, the South East −42.8 per cent, and Scotland −39.3 per cent – whereas East Anglia and Wales show reductions of less than 10 per cent. These sectors are the ones that as a whole declined least – they provided something of a cushion against job loss in certain places; that is, a useful element of 'diversification'. They also tended to have spread from the 'axial belt' of industry to smaller adjoining regions, notably contributing to relatively better trends in the East Midlands, East Anglia, the South West and Wales.

We should now ask how far the changes of this period were predetermined by the different industrial structure of the different regions at the starting point of 1971. As in Chapter 3 it is possible to calculate what would have happened if every narrowly-defined industry in every region had increased or decreased at its *national* rate, and then to compare the total number of jobs actually filled. Calculations at different levels of detail show three regions consistently performing *worse* than forecast in industry: the South East, the North West and Scotland. Three regions consistently perform much *better* than forecast: these are the relatively more rural areas, the East Midlands, East Anglia and the South West.

Not surprisingly when we turn to *total* employment trends in industry (Fig. 5.3), we find these same three regions are the most successful.

Fig.5.3 Total employment change in industry, 1971–91.

*Source:* NOMIS.

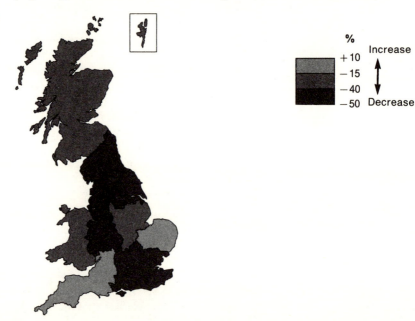

%
+ 10    Increase
− 15
− 40
− 50    Decrease

### The role of individual companies

The overall trends described above involve in reality a great variety of events in different industries. Chapter 4 examined the role of individual companies in periods of growth. It is possible now to ask what part they play in periods of decline. Factors in the past development of a multi-plant company may have a bearing on particular decisions whether or not to close an individual factory. Continuing the comments of the last chapter, Fig. 5.4 maps ICI's numbers of UK employees at the end of 1976 and 1990. In such a large company it is possible to see whether staffing levels in all the divisions fell in line with the wider trends that were studied above.

Fig.5.4 Employment change in ICI (UK), 1976–90.

*Source:* ICI.

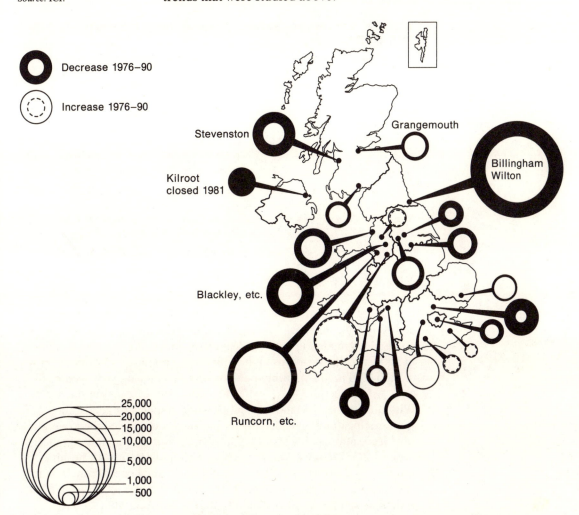

Decrease 1976–90

Increase 1976–90

Stevenston

Grangemouth

Billingham Wilton

Kilroot closed 1981

Blackley, etc.

Runcorn, etc.

25,000
20,000
15,000
10,000
5,000
1,000
500

By and large they did. From 1976 to 1990 the total number of ICI employees at the UK locations (Fig. 5.4) fell by no less than 35,200, from 82,500 to 47,300, a very large drop of 42.6 per cent. There were six major sites which were abandoned in the period, notably ICI's one factory in Northern Ireland, at Kilroot. Established only in 1958, this was one of a number of factories set up by multi-plant companies to make artificial fibres in that province. All were closed in the early 1980s

51

recession when the price of their raw materials rose excessively. ICI also closed three sites in North West England and one at Stevenage New Town in the South East. In general, however, Fig. 5.4 shows large percentage reductions at nearly all locations, including one of 46.9 per cent, involving 10,700 job losses, in Cleveland. Only four showed any increase in employees. It is possible to classify job losses in any industry into three types. Closures (full or partial) fall unevenly between locations and can be described as *rationalisation*. On the other hand, the very general policy of maintaining output with reduced staff, affecting 29 locations in ICI, can be called *intensification*. Where output is replaced at a fresh site with new plant, this form of job loss is known as *investment and technical change*.

**Table 5.2    Employment decline in Imperial Chemical Industries (ICI) UK, 1976–90 (December)**

| | Main locations | | Employees 1976 | | 1990 | Change, 1976–90 | |
|---|---|---|---|---|---|---|---|
| | 1976 | 1990 | Nos. | % monthly paid | Nos. | Nos. | % |
| North | 27 | 22 | 69,800 | 35.7 | 39,000 | −30,800 | −44.1 |
| South | 12 | 11 | 12,700 | 58.1 | 8,300 | −4,400 | −34.6 |
| Total | 39 | 33 | 82,500 | 39.1 | 47,300 | −35,200 | −42.7 |

*Notes:* 'North' comprises Northern Ireland, Scotland, Wales, the Northern Region, North West England, Yorkshire and Humberside, and the West Midlands.

'South' comprises the South East, South West, East Anglia and the East Midlands.

*Source:* ICI headquarters, London.

As mentioned earlier, ICI has been forced to reduce its dependence on heavy bulk chemicals and replace them with more refined specialist goods. This reduction yields a clear lesson in location trends. As shown in Table 5.2, the locations in the south had a majority – 58.1 per cent – of their staff in the 'monthly-paid' or white-collar category, whereas only just over a third – 35.7 per cent – fell in this category in the north. With the emphasis on more scientific work in specialist goods, the southern locations provided higher incomes and reduced their overall workforce appreciably less than those in the north. The only significant expansion in the north was in the pharmaceutical group in Cheshire, where a majority of its staff are monthly-paid and benefit from its rural environment as a place to live. On the whole it is correct to speak of a widening 'spatial division of labour' in ICI, between white-collar, research, administrative and clerical tasks concentrated in the south, and the more routine bulk processing continuing in the north, where, as in industry at large, the labour force fell more rapidly. At the same time, it can be said that ICI was contributing to the 'international division of labour' through establishing plants abroad, where its workforce has been increasing. In the four years 1986 to 1990, for example, its overseas employees increased from 65,000 to 78,400, or 59.3 per cent of the ICI world total.

## Selection of factories for closure

The fate of many towns hangs on the decisions of multi-plant companies whether to expand, contract or close local branches. The local council, concerned by local workers' and business fears, may try to foresee the chances of closure. In the case mentioned above, of ICI's closure of its plant at Kilroot in Northern Ireland, the whole basis of its production of artificial fibres had become uneconomic. In other cases, however, the need to cut output across a range of fairly similar plants may mean that there is a selection that must be made. External factors or internal conditions leave it obvious which plant should be closed on possibly a quarter of occasions. In the rest, there is a need for the multi-plant company to make a choice from alternative plants in different places. Often it must weigh several factors of varying merit.

Geographers have classified these deciding factors into four types. The first is the *role of the factory* in terms of its size, product, adaptability and range. When there is spare capacity in several plants, the output of a small factory can easily be fitted within a larger one. It is often the relative size or role of the factory that is important, in particular whether it is central or not to the activities of the main business and has any headquarters functions in the control of other plants. A second aspect is that of *operational factors*, such as poor labour productivity, management or machinery, which would clearly recommend a factory for closure on normal commercial grounds. A third factor is that of *location*, comprising geographers' traditional concern over transport costs and remoteness, the distance in travel time between the company headquarters and the factory, and the availability of government grants in 'assisted areas'. Fourthly, *property factors* may be important, in terms of a limited site or poorly-designed unit.

**Table 5.3    Major factors in selecting a plant for closure 1980–86, and percentages of jobs lost (1980) in 118 plant closures**

|  | Northern Ireland | Tyneside | South Hampshire | Leicestershire |
|---|---|---|---|---|
| Role of factory | 69 | 89 | 53 | 85 |
| Location | 17 | 22 | 32 | 19 |
| Operational factors | 27 | 9 | 14 | 0 |
| Property factors | 2 | 0 | 56 | 36 |

*Source:* Fothergill and Guy (1990).

Surveys of these factors suggest that a branch plant or a 'subsidiary' (a firm which has been acquired by another) is much more likely to close than are independent or headquarters plants. In turn, research in the UK in the period 1976–81 confirmed the often-stated view that 'firms close their branch factories first' – that is, before leading, well-established plants. Work on 118 branch plant closures in four subregions of the UK between 1980 and 1986 is summarised in Table 5.3. Because the 118 factories varied in size, the table shows the proportions of total jobs affected by the closure decision under four factors.

Among the four types of factor which were mentioned above, the *role of the factory* is of outstanding importance (although it is not the leading factor in South Hampshire). In addition to questions of plant size, product and capability, the disadvantage of lying outside the mainstream of the company's business was significant in all areas. This can arise where a company has been acquired as part of a merger with a bigger one. The table shows *operational factors* to be important in Northern Ireland, but it is *location* which takes second place in the table, dominated by the remoteness of plants in Northern Ireland and Tyneside, and the lack of government grants in South Hampshire and Leicestershire. These last two areas also had nearly all the closures due to *property factors*, chiefly the lack of expansion land in closely built-up areas.

## Policy significance of these results

The results are of great importance for the geographer and for regional policy. They show that location and local economic conditions were not the leading factors to blame for the many branch factory closures by multi-plant companies in the 1980s. 'Location' was a major factor in less than a quarter of the closure decisions affecting Northern Ireland and Tyneside. There was some indication that productivity and attitudes to work were of importance in Northern Ireland closures. In three-quarters of the job losses, however, it was the 'role of the factory' which was more important than its operation or location. The implication of these results is that the 'assisted areas' of the north are not of themselves uneconomic places to build or retain a factory.

It is necessary to ask how these results can be reconciled with the incidence during the 1980s of even greater job losses in the north than would be accounted for by their industrial structure. There were more closures among branch factories than would strictly be expected. The answer is that all factories go through expansion and decline. Many peripheral coalfield areas and Northern Ireland received a lot of new factories of multi-plant corporations during the heyday of regional policy in the 1960s, but, 20 years later, in the 1980s, these same plants tended to be at the stage of losing markets.

## Job loss in the later 1980s

Conditions changed somewhat in the second half of the 1980s, and there was a small net gain of factory jobs from new investment in parts of the north but not in the south. This contrast indicated that the massive de-industrialisation of the north, which was such a prevalent feature from 1976 to 1986, had been arrested for the time being. By 1988, redundancies had shrunk to a low level in most industries, including iron and steel, chemicals and vehicles. In 1989 redundancies continued at the rate of half a million people per year losing their jobs compulsorily (before a renewed increase). A survey revealed that these job losses were still concentrated among male manual factory workers in the north. Manual workers faced two-and-a-half times the rate of redundancies of non-manual workers. The rate for male employees was almost twice as high as for females. In manufacturing, the likelihood of redundancy was almost three times as high as in the service sector. It appeared that the North West, Yorkshire and Humberside and Scotland were the areas worst affected.

As mentioned earlier, coal-mining suffered severely in all regions. In general, job losses were heavy in nationalised sectors, both in preparation for privatisation and in the wake of it. At the end of the period, only a few industries were immune from further reductions. Multi-plant corporations making computers, electrical goods, motor vehicles and clothing were forced to rationalise and automate further their operations. The highest rates of factory job loss, 1986–91, were in textiles, motor vehicles, aerospace and shipbuilding.

A new feature of this period was that,the improved international relations reduced the need for new defence equipment of all kinds. In the early 1980s the making of military aircraft, radar systems, naval vessels, submarines and tanks had buttressed the economy of several areas including some northern shipyards. However, by 1991 the reduction of defence orders was beginning to undermine the survival of large companies in the south. Geographers had calculated that 68 per cent of defence spending was there, and it is clear that further cuts will add to the de-industrialisation of southern areas. Combining this and all other factors, engineering was expected to lose about 10 per cent of its two million jobs between 1990 and the year 2000.

## Conclusion

Inequalities of economic development and social well-being between British regions today suggest a division between a poorer north and a wealthier south. Table 5.4 amalgamates the regions used in the maps of this chapter into these two groups (excluding Northern Ireland), and their composition is shown. Wales, the West Midlands, Yorkshire and

**Table 5.4   Employment decline in industry, by two divisions of Great Britain, 1971–91 (thousands)**

|  | Employees | | Change, 1971–91 | |
|  | 1971 | 1991 | Numbers | % |
|---|---|---|---|---|
| North | 4,998 | 2,822 | −2,176 | −43.5 |
| South | 3,704 | 2,373 | −1,331 | −35.9 |
| Total | 8,702 | 5,195 | −3,507 | −40.3 |

*Notes:* 'North' comprises Scotland, Wales, the Northern Region, North West England, Yorkshire and Humberside, and the West Midlands.

'South' comprises the South East, South West, East Anglia and the East Midlands.

*Source:* NOMIS (National Online Manpower Information System); excludes agriculture and services.

Humberside and areas to the north of them have the majority of the country's industrial workers. The maps of this chapter have shown that there are variations within the northern regions. In certain industries, the South East performed as badly as the north. In some industries that were new to them, Wales and other northern regions did relatively well. In the first part of the 1970s, and in the late 1980s, the north as a whole did marginally better than the south.

None the less, the total of industrial jobs was reduced over 20 years by 2.1 million (42.6 per cent) in the north compared with 1.3 million (34.8 per cent) in the south. These proportions are very similar to the experience of ICI over 16 years. These north–south differences are highly significant. The decline of the north is due above all to the overall national reduction in industrial jobs, based both on international trends and on Britain's unique halt in the growth of industrial output from 1974 to 1988. The relatively greater decline of the north's industrial jobs is due to three factors. The most important was the structure of industry itself, biased still towards relatively greater decline (given the weight of the heavier coalfield-based industries which had already caused difficulties between the wars). This was aggravated by a second factor, the wide range of measures used by the Conservative government from 1979 onwards to rationalise the nationalised industries which it inherited, namely coal, iron and steel and shipbuilding. The third factor, however, was that multi-plant private companies, British and foreign, made decisions about closing pre-war and post-war factories which appeared to discriminate against northern branches. The remoteness of the north and poor productivity played some part in certain cases, but the overwhelming proportion of closure decisions can be attributed to the allotted role of individual branches in the overall organisation.

Beyond these factors, however, is the point that the northern industrial areas had relatively few other 'strings to their bow'. They depended heavily on industry for their jobs. The rate of industrial job loss was also very significant in the south, and indeed caused serious unemployment in inner areas of London and larger towns. For much of the 20 years, however, the south enjoyed a large share of the growth of another sector, that of services such as banking and finance, which are the subject of the next chapter.

It is therefore to industrial job loss that we should attribute the continuing high levels of unemployment at the beginning of the 1990s. In terms of the proportions of the workforce who were unemployed at mid-1992, the worst employment conditions were met in Northern Ireland, the Northern Region and the North West, particularly in the coastal conurbations identified as problem areas nearly 60 years earlier. The effect of general de-industrialisation had been to spread similar conditions over much of the north.

# 6   The role of the service sector

**Introduction**

What characterises the most prosperous areas of Britain is a high dependence not on manufacturing but on providing services. It is in these areas that people have generally avoided unemployment, by transferring from the manufacturing to the service sectors. At some times and in some places the growth of activity in the service sector has exceeded the reduction of jobs in manufacturing and drawn workers and other resources away from it. The competition for staff and for office sites has driven factories to move away from parts of London and the surrounding counties. While this book has seen manufacturing industry as the prime determinant of regional growth, it is now possible to think of a region's development being *led by services* into a 'post-industrial' future.

## The definition of services

One dictionary definition of 'service' is 'an organized system of labour and material aids used to supply the needs of the public', such as a telephone service or bus service (*Collins Dictionary of the English Language*, 1986). The same entry supplies 26 other definitions, referring to the supply, installation or maintenance of goods, to vehicle maintenance, to catering work in hotels or restaurants, and to work in the civil service and armed forces. All these activities fall within the scope of this chapter. The reader may feel that the 'service sector' is something of a rag-bag. Indeed it is best defined as including all economic activities other than the *production* of goods. The components are disparate and may be grouped together in many different ways. What the geographer must do, however, is to identify those activities which – as is normal for the production of goods – are provided *by one area for another*. The growth of such trade brings in payments which support the development of the supply areas. This represents the growth of 'service exports', or of 'invisible exports', from an area.

## Service exports

Many white-collar workers in the City of London and elsewhere are paid to produce services for the rest of the world. These are so important that the proceeds of 'invisible exports', from insurance, banking, finance, shipping, airline and tourist transactions, are counted in the regular statements of the country's financial balance of payments. The same kind of dealings take place *within* Britain. The provision of services to other regions may be crucial to understanding the invisible balance of trade of a British region, and therefore its total income and economy. A firm providing a service, for example shipping, is important. It adds to the number of jobs in the region directly through

57

The City of London is one of the major service centres of the world, dealing with banking, finance, shipping and all types of insurance transactions.

the firm's local spending and its payment of salaries and wages, and indirectly through employees' spending on other goods and services. It thus supports a part of the total population of its area.

This concept of service exports is already to be found in geography textbooks. It was recognised at an early stage that service industries *may* earn their livelihood from distant markets (at home or overseas), and may therefore choose a location independently of other sectors. The role of wider markets was seen as providing capital cities, international ports, financial centres and tourist resorts with just as valid an 'economic base' for urban growth as manufacturing areas. Thus traditional texts saw London's role as being based partly on the work of government, as was that of Washington, DC, Paris or Moscow. They saw entrepôts (exchange ports) like London, Rotterdam or Singapore as gaining a significant part of their income from shipping activity for other countries. Financial centres such as London, New York, Zurich or Milan provided much of their own income from the profits of money transactions. Finally, areas such as the south coast of England developed large towns mainly engaged in receiving seaside summer visitors, comparable to some extent with the tourist industries of Alpine Switzerland or the south of France.

Service exports as viewed by the geographer have now broadened in type, range and complexity. A present-day example from each of the main parts of the service sector, in Britain and the rest of the European Community, is provided in Table 6.1. Except in tourism, the examples of major service growth tend to come from leading cities, and in the UK from London and the South East.

**Table 6.1   Some examples in which states or major regions derive 'basic' income from provision of services**

| Service sector | UK regional examples | EC examples |
|---|---|---|
| Construction | London (international consultancy firms) | Rome (international consultancy firms) |
| Hotels and catering | South-west England (tourist industry) | Costa Brava (tourist industry) |
| Wholesale distribution | North-west England (mail-order depots) | Europoort, Netherlands (oil storage and distribution) |
| Retail distribution | London, Oxford Street (international visitor sales) | Paris (international visitor sales) |
| Transport and communication | London airports (international transit trade) | Athens (income from ship-owning) |
| Business services, including banking, insurance and finance | Edinburgh (financial centre) | Frankfurt (financial centre) |
| Public administration and defence | Cardiff (county and Welsh administrative centre) | Brussels (national and international administrative centre) |
| Education and health | London, Harley Street (international medical visits) | Florence (international university) |
| Other services | Liverpool (Littlewoods Pools) | Rome (national and international Church administration and pilgrimage) |

## Four kinds of services

The identification of service export activities on the ground is helped by a number of distinctions. 'Producer services' comprise activities, such as those of specialist banks, for example, that are provided for other firms and public agencies, within the overall system of production of goods and services. 'Consumer services' are those provided for ordinary customers who are often more local. Thus the scope for developing producer services underlies the question whether other UK regions can increase their service sector activity as rapidly as the South East.

The question can be approached by classifying service establishments, as they exist on the ground, into four types. Figure 6.1 illustrates and utilises the four types, labelled as CNB, CB, PNB and PB. The first distinction at Figure 6.1a is between producer services (P) and consumer services (C). The second division is of a different kind and lies between services provided for users in the same geographical area of study, the 'non-basic' sector (NB), and for those in the rest of the country or the world, the basic sector (B).

In manufacturing or services, activity is deemed to be 'basic' if it generates income from outside the area of study. To the extent, for example, that the tourist industry of South West England attracts spending visitors from the South East, the Midlands, Northern England,

Fig.6.1 The structure of modern services in the local economy.

**a Four types of service establishment**

|  | NON-BASIC (NB) for customers in area of study | BASIC (B) for customers in other areas |
|---|---|---|
| CONSUMER SERVICES (C) for ordinary members of the population | CNB e.g. a supermarket | CB e.g. tourism |
| PRODUCER SERVICES (P) for business customers in any sector | PNB e.g. a local road haulier | PB e.g. a national merchant bank headquarters |

**b Different manufacturing:service ratios**

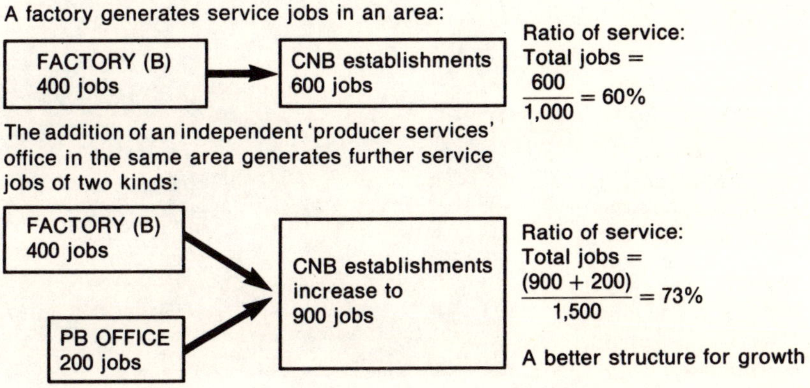

A factory generates service jobs in an area:

FACTORY (B) 400 jobs → CNB establishments 600 jobs

Ratio of service:
Total jobs =
$$\frac{600}{1,000} = 60\%$$

The addition of an independent 'producer services' office in the same area generates further service jobs of two kinds:

FACTORY (B) 400 jobs
PB OFFICE 200 jobs
→ CNB establishments increase to 900 jobs

Ratio of service:
Total jobs =
$$\frac{(900 + 200)}{1,500} = 73\%$$

A better structure for growth

59

or other areas of Britain or the world, and not from within its own boundaries, it is seen to be 'basic' to the growth of the region. This is, unusually, a consumer industry which brings in income and can be described as 'consumer basic' (CB). Visitors' spending in hotels, restaurants, etc. is partly devoted to paying firms and workers in the region. That income, like that of most factories, is in turn spent mainly on non-basic services provided in the area, and thus generates the normal range of schools, hospitals, supermarkets and other local market services found in nearly all parts of Britain. These are 'non-basic' (CNB) because they do not of themselves attract income to the area and are not therefore involved directly in supporting its population. A non-basic establishment in producer services (PNB), for instance a local road haulier, is also distinctive. It would have to expand its customer market area over large distances to generate many new jobs for its area as part of the basic sector and to become a basic producer services activity (PB). The scope for such extensions is generally much greater in producer than in consumer services.

### Variation in the service composition of areas

It is the different mixing of these types, especially the presence in an area of PB, a basic producer service such as international banking, which produces markedly varying ratios of service to total employment from area to area. These ratios are important in determining whether or not a region will enjoy its full share of the national growth of a service-rich, post-industrial economy.

Figure 6.1b demonstrates in the top line the normal view of the relationship of factory to local consumer service (CNB) jobs. Earnings in the factory generate further jobs as its wage packets and salaries are spent in the same area, and this mechanism is called a 'multiplier'. Changes in the national economy mean that these multiplier ratios have

The head office of a national organisation like the Halifax Building Society in the north of England brings jobs to the region, and attracts other services to the same area.

increased over time; Fig. 6.1b assumes that the factory, which is the 'basic' employer, bringing jobs into the area in the first place, generates three additional jobs for every two that it provides directly.

The addition of a 'producer services' office with sales outside the area (PB) is illustrated in the last part of the figure. Like the factory, it generates additions to and expansions of the CNB establishments (the same multiplier of 1.5 can be assumed here). However, in statistics for the area, this office will be counted in with all the other service establishments. Total service employment will account for 1,100 out of the 1,500 jobs in the area, or 73 per cent of the total, compared with 60 per cent before the addition of this office.

The proportion of service jobs in the real-world economy varied in 1991 between 61 per cent in the East Midlands and 78 per cent in the South East of England (Fig. 6.2a). Much of this variation depends, as in Fig. 6.1b, on the admixture of producer services office jobs as additions to the more long-established primary sector and manufacturing jobs of the different regions, as well as on the continuation of the tourist trade in the South West and some other regions.

Fig.6.2 (a) Service employment and its principal centres. (b) The British employment pattern of a leading accountancy company: Price Waterhouse, 1984.

*Source:* Price Waterhouse.

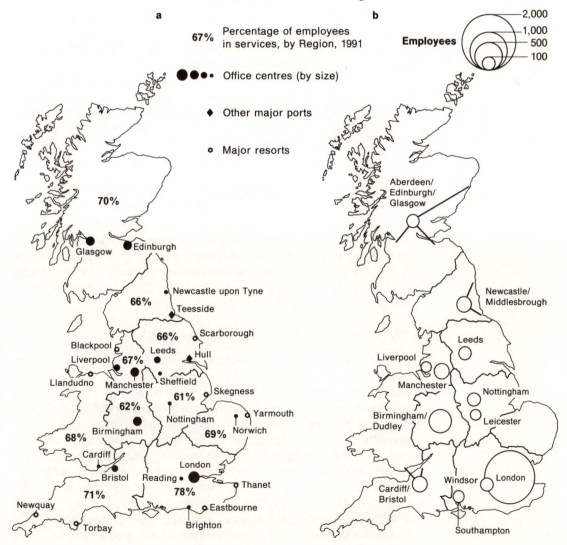

It is true that some office jobs are found even in the smallest market town as well as in most suburban high streets. Most larger towns have branches of all major banks and building societies as well as the government departments which are represented outside London. The main *regional office centres* are marked on Fig. 6.2a, although Fig. 6.2b shows additional offices in a large accountancy firm. To provide many jobs, however, a local office has to expand beyond the regional scale of operation. Thus the Halifax and Norwich Union Building Societies, for example, have expanded from their original bases to provide a large number of jobs, including normally many for school-leavers, by undertaking national-scale work from Halifax and Norwich by post.

## The growth of services

The volume of export producer services in the South East is so great as to deserve special attention. The financial activities of the City of London pre-date British industrialism, having originated to serve the large volume of government borrowing in the eighteenth century to pay for Britain's foreign wars. The growth of imperial functions in the administration of a large part of the world, as colonies or as exporting areas of minerals and food, added greatly to the wealthy population of the growing city. In fact, south-east England developed a high dependence on financial, trading, wholesaling, shipping and political services in the nineteenth century while the rest of the UK was occupied with the Industrial Revolution. Including families who established large country houses in the 'home counties' around London, the region developed great wealth almost independently of the industrial north. Much of this wealth was spent on services provided by a large working population.

Already by 1841, at least 40 per cent of employment in south-east England lay in the service sector. From 1901 to 1971 the figure stood close to 60 per cent before expanding to 78 per cent by 1991. In 1989, 74 per cent of the value of production in the region was undertaken by the service sector, led by financial and business services. In that year, 68 per cent of UK civilian employment lay in the service sector, compared with figures of 67 to 69 per cent in the Netherlands, Denmark, Norway and Sweden, and 71 per cent in the USA.

### The growth of service activities internationally

So we now see the fulfilment of earlier predictions that advanced nations would increase the size of their service sector to 70 per cent of total employment. This proportion represents the final 'stage' of a progression which begins with an undeveloped country in which 70 per cent of workers may be found in the primary sectors (principally agriculture, but also forestry, fishing and mining). *If* industrialisation occurs, then the workforce will move into both manufacturing and service activities. In 'mature' industrial countries, however, a further shift occurs from manufacturing to services, which may, as in Britain, be accentuated by a period of 'de-industrialisation' (Chapter 5).

Why these changes should occur, however, is not obvious. One traditional view was that increasing efficiency and productivity of *industry* would yield higher incomes for its workers. These higher incomes would be spent in increasing proportions on services, whether as transport, leisure, education or health. A second part of the explanation is that most services were not and are not, it was said, capable of the same improvements in productivity; they would therefore need proportionately more workers than manufacturing to keep up with demand. However, more precise attempts to measure the productivity of services have cast doubt on this view. There is no firm evidence that productivity rises more slowly in the service sector and this part of the explanation is therefore weaker. On closer examination the sequence of expansion in the service sector varies between different countries, although a part of its work is everywhere low paid.

One reason why the ratio of service to manufacturing employment increased so markedly in Britain in the 1980s was that consumers increasingly purchased foreign-manufactured goods, whereas most services, other than foreign holidays, were provided at home. In turn, however, another reason has emerged for manufacturing firms to reduce their labour force. They have increasingly replaced their internal services such as accounting, legal work, market research, catering and cleaning by 'buying in' the work of specialist firms, which are naturally classified in the service sector (the internal employees were under 'manufacturing').

### The basis of world cities like London

London's disproportionate growth reflects both its past and its recent international significance. It is firmly seen to be one of the world's three leading financial centres together with Tokyo (Japan) and New York (USA); their three working days in different time zones together span the 24-hour day. As such, London is at the time of writing pre-eminent over the rival European financial centres such as Frankfurt (Germany) and Paris (France).

It is valuable to ask what creates and sustains such international centres of white-collar work. An exile from Europe, the geographer Jean Gottmann, was so impressed by New York's command of the north-eastern seaboard of the USA that he named the whole area 'megalopolis' ('a very large city'). The region had taken on a new shape on the map because it was increasingly dominated by functions of the urban service sector, particularly in finance and politics. The origins of New York's role went back three centuries and lay in its key port location rather than in resources. The initial creation of its many office jobs began a cumulative process of growth.

London can be seen in the same light in the combination of historical port and office functions. Translated to the circumstances of today, however, the activity of handling goods in the Thames has been relegated in importance to the information-handling activities of the City of London, in producer services, and of Westminster, in politics and administration. Every kind of highly specialist business service is provided in the City, while Westminster houses offices representing virtually every political interest in the country. Geographers are convinced, from studying senior office workers' diaries and movements, that it is the opportunity for face-to-face contacts in meetings which makes a central London location so important. But in turn it is the communications network of London, as of New York, that enhances the opportunity for face-to-face contact by also providing convenient meetings with business visitors from elsewhere. Because the fastest and most frequent rail and air links focus on London (compared, say, with Birmingham) it has a high level of 'contact potential'.

There are threats to London's survival from its internal congestion, and from the financial changes in the European Community. However, a most obvious question is whether improvements in telecommunications have not been so great that much of the work could be done elsewhere, avoiding the heavy rents paid for London premises, and possibly restoring some balance to inter-regional development.

Heathrow, London's main airport, is a focus of world communications, ensuring that London continues to be a convenient meeting place for business people from all over the world.

### Office decentralisation from London

The transplanting of offices from central London has in fact already added considerably to the economic structure of some British provincial towns. These transfers sometimes leave undisturbed the national or international scope of the London head office, but take over its more routine functions, such as data processing or records. This 'back office' enjoys cheaper rents and labour, while a London office is retained for the high-level decision-making meetings of senior staff.

There were precedents for the removal of government offices from London in the Second World War. The administration of post-war state pensions and national insurance was centralised at new offices at Longbenton, near Newcastle upon Tyne, now the Department of Social Security. As mentioned at the end of Chapter 3, however, shortages of land, labour and transport facilities in London were found to be pushing more offices towards decentralisation by the 1960s. The government established the Location of Offices Bureau (1963–79), to encourage firms to leave London, and also took steps to remove civil service office work from central London. It had been hoped that, like factories under regional policy, offices could be induced to move well beyond the boundaries of the South East.

There were a few cases of longer-distance movements of large offices to the north of England. Examples include the Giro Bank, located at

Fig.6.3 Office moves
from central London,
1964–92.

*Source:* Location of Offices
Bureau, JLW Consulting and
Research.

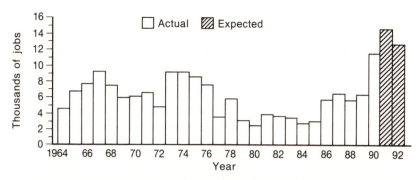

Bootle, Merseyside, and the Department of Education and Science's
statistics work at Darlington, County Durham. However, the great
majority of office moves occurring in the period 1965–76 (Fig. 6.3) were
found to be to the rest of Greater London and the South East.
Compared with the manufacturing sector where only a few key
managers and workers needed to transfer to a new branch, it was found
that 25 to 40 per cent of employees needed to transfer with an office to
secure its continued viability. Office messengers frequently transported
papers between London and the new office, generally restricting
distances to 1½ to 2 hours' travelling time. An example was the
establishment of Barclaycard at Northampton. Thus private offices were
found to be *less* mobile than manufacturing; if they did move beyond the
boundaries of the South East, it was to attractive cities of adjoining
areas such as Bristol, Cambridge, Northampton and Norwich.

Improved telecommunications in the 1980s did not replace the need
for face-to-face meetings in London. The growth of financial office jobs
in London in the second half of the decade prompted greater mobility in
office locations at its end. Figure 6.4 demonstrates an increased
tendency for the pressure of development in the South East then to
displace firms to the South West and Midlands. The same pressures
prompted a revival of the decentralisation of government offices, which
account for several of the 'scheduled moves, 1991', notably to the East
Midlands and Yorkshire and Humberside. (These locations provide an
effective compromise between the advantages of labour supply and the
problems of distance from London.)

Fig.6.4 Destination of
offices decentralising
from central London into
the rest of the UK,
outside the South East,
since 1983.

*Source:* Location of Offices
Bureau, JLW Consulting and
Research, November 1991.

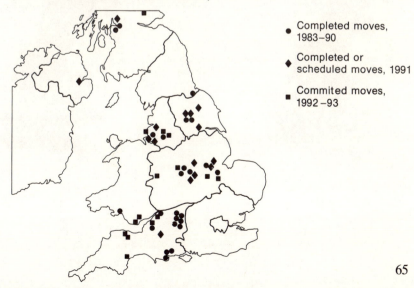

# The overall regional pattern of service employment, 1971–91

Fig.6.5 Employment change in services, 1971–91. (The four sectors shown here add up to make the total that is shown in Fig. 6.6.)

*Source:* NOMIS.

The relocation of offices *and* their subsequent growth are included in Fig. 6.5, which divides up the service sector to match the statistics of Table 6.2. It must be borne in mind that the growth of employment includes both that of important 'basic' services, and those changes in 'non-basic' employment which are due directly to the growth or decline of population and of employment in *other* industries and services.

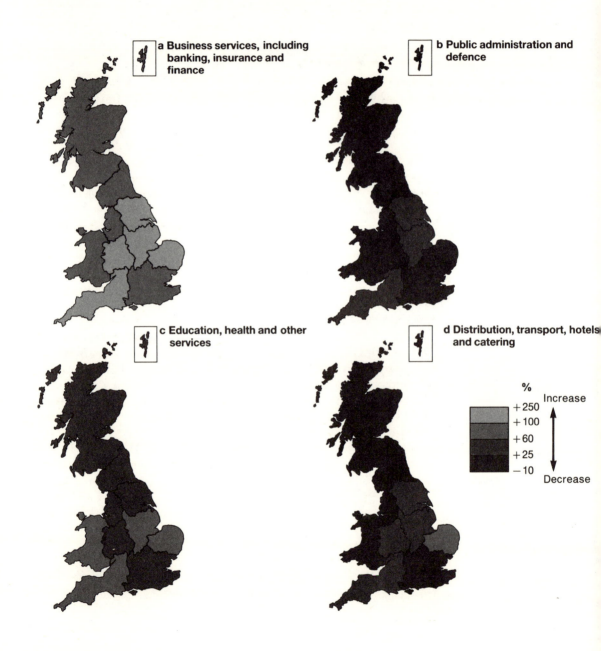

a Business services, including banking, insurance and finance

b Public administration and defence

c Education, health and other services

d Distribution, transport, hotels and catering

%
Increase
+ 250
+ 100
+ 60
+ 25
− 10
Decrease

**Table 6.2  Employment increase in services, by leading sectors, Great Britain 1971–91 (thousands)**

|  | Employees | | Change, 1971–91 | |
|---|---|---|---|---|
|  | 1971 | 1991 | Numbers | % |
| Business services, including banking, insurance and finance | 1,318 | 2,595 | +1,277 | +96.9 |
| Public administration and defence | 1,730 | 1,890 | +160 | +9.2 |
| Education, health and other services | 3,189 | 4,844 | +1,655 | +51.9 |
| Distribution, transport, hotels and catering | 5,135 | 5,908 | +773 | +15.1 |
| Total | 11,372 | 15,237 | +3,865 | +34.0 |

*Source:* Official figures via NOMIS (National Online Manpower Information System, University of Durham).

Figure 6.5a is dealing with virtually a doubling of employment. Of the gain of 1.3 million jobs in business services, nearly half (580,000) occurred in South East England. None the less, the rate of expansion was higher – over 100 per cent – in the four surrounding regions and in Yorkshire and Humberside. This represents the decentralisation of private offices across the boundaries of the South East to centres such as Bristol, Coventry, Northampton and Norwich, as well as the dispersal and growth of population requiring 'non-basic' services.

Figure 6.5b shows systematically lower rates of increase because public sector service employment lost its lead to the private sector in the 1980s. In the 1970s, policy led to the withdrawal of 24,000 civil service jobs from London, and their replacement in peripheral regions in centres such as Swansea and Liverpool. In the 1980s, the South East continued to lose national government jobs, though principally to the adjoining regions.

Figure 6.5c relates to the very largest increase of jobs, of no less than 1.7 million, in education, health and other services. The map represents increased standards of provision which are reflected in job increases in all regions of Britain. The higher rates of growth, however, are shown to have occurred in precisely the regions of greatest population growth. This suggests that these services are related to people's needs arising within their regional boundaries, and that these services are not 'basic' to the regional economies.

Figure 6.5d is the most general in character of the four. It reflects a north–south divide between slow rates of increase in the north and faster ones in the south, with the exception of the South East. These categories of service employment expanded by more than 40 per cent in East Anglia, the East Midlands and the South West. Taking all categories of service employment together (Fig. 6.6a) it is again found that these three areas are the leaders, together with Yorkshire and Humberside.

Fig.6.6 Change in
employment, 1971–91.

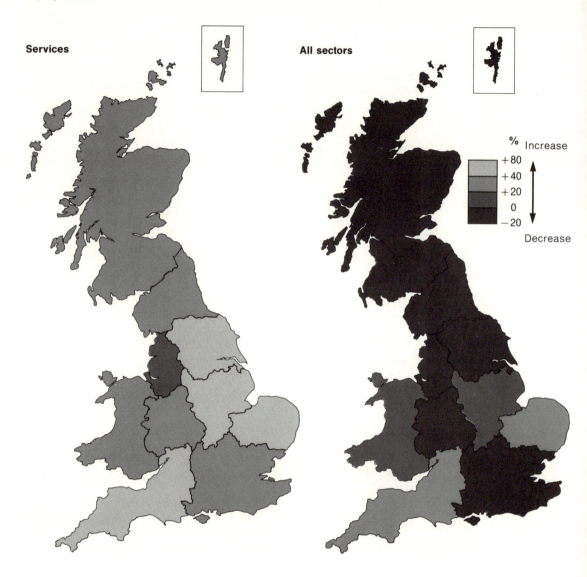

## Conclusion

The broad picture of the economy over the 20 years 1971–91 was that
services (Fig. 6.6a) contributed to a deepening of the north–south
divide. The decentralisation of producer services in the movement of
offices from London and the South East contributed to the population
growth of three adjoining regions. That in turn led to further growth of
mainly non-basic services such as retailing, health and education. At the
same time, the lesser growth of income and population led to much
lower increases in several northern regions, including a reduction of
retail jobs in the Northern and North West regions, and a reduction of
transport jobs in many areas.

**Table 6.3    Employment change in all sectors, by two divisions of Great Britain 1971–91 (thousands)**

|  | Employees | | Change, 1971–91 | |
|---|---|---|---|---|
|  | 1971 | 1991 | Numbers | % |
| North | 11,016 | 10,270 | −746 | −6.8 |
| South | 10,637 | 11,397 | +760 | +7.1 |
| Total | 21,653 | 21,667 | +14 | +0.1 |

*Notes:* 'North' comprises Scotland, Wales, the Northern Region, North West England, Yorkshire and Humberside and the West Midlands.

'South' comprises the South East, South West, East Anglia and the East Midlands.

*Source:* NOMIS.

The contribution of service jobs, together with agriculture and industry, is crucial in deciding the overall pattern of employment change. Figure 6.6b firmly places East Anglia and the South West in the leading position for economic growth, with 30 per cent more jobs in 1991 than 1971, followed by the East Midlands with 13 per cent more. The Northern and North West regions lost more than 10 per cent of all jobs. It is sometimes argued that the growth of service jobs fails to compensate for the loss of jobs in other sectors because a considerable number of them are held by females and are more poorly paid than are male jobs. Over these particular 20 years the small gain of only 14,000 employees in employment hides a gain of 2.13 million female jobs in the economy at large and a loss of 2.11 million male jobs. Such was the pace of de-industrialisation in this period that all the regions except East Anglia and the South West had fewer male jobs in 1991 than 1971. Table 6.3 shows that over the 20-year period the south gained just over three-quarters of a million jobs – 7 per cent of the 1971 total – and the north lost slightly fewer.

These features point to the need for closer study of the more recent growth sectors in the next chapter, and of a shift in the economy from urban to rural regions in the last chapter of the book.

# 7 Growth sectors of the 1980s

## The nature of economic change in the decade

In the 1980s a pattern of growth sectors emerged which deepened the 'north–south divide'. The period after the severe industrial recession of 1979–81 took on distinct characteristics. Multi-plant companies closed factories or reduced their size. Industrial areas, mainly in the north, suffered the worst. Ever since then, the important question has been whether such 'de-industrialised' areas could recover, through the growth of small business or by renewed investment from outside, or whether southern areas would increasingly dominate the growth of a 'post-industrial' country.

The answer was clear, at least until the next recession of 1990–92. The nature of the economy shifted more favourably to the south. Table 7.1 illustrates the favoured and less favoured activities on the economic map. The entries of each column overlap each other, but the left- and right-hand columns could be said to characterise the south and the north respectively. In the 1980s growth was slow in returning to northern industrial areas. The decade ended with fewer male workers and fewer factory workers than when it began. A town which started the decade with a bias towards small firms working in the private sector had a better likelihood of ending the decade with some growth and a larger population. The favoured characteristics were those of southern areas of Britain.

**Table 7.1 Elements of economic activity that were favourably and less favourably placed in trends of the 1980s**

| Favoured | Unfavoured |
|---|---|
| Service sector | Manufacturing sector |
| Small firms, without trade unions | Large trade-union-dominated establishments |
| Private sector | Public sector |
| White-collar work | Manual work |
| Female employment | Male employment |
| Part-time employment | Full-time employment |
| Self-employed | Employees |

To understand why the advantages of the south were generally strengthened, we must look at changes in the overall nature of the economy. Figure 7.1 measures expansion in several main sectors from 1980 to 1990 (the shaded area of each bar), and in the previous decade, and provides a forecast to the year 2000. There was an increase in the value of production in manufacturing, but this was, unusually, not much more than in the 'distribution' sector, which included investment in new

Fig.7.1 Changes in the value of production in different principal sectors in the UK, 1971–2000.

*Source:* Cambridge Econometrics, 1992.

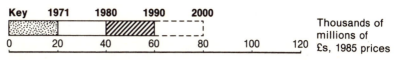
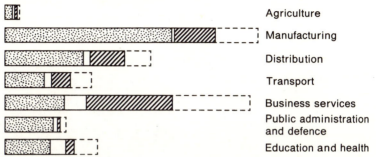

supermarkets and hypermarkets. The public sectors of administration, defence, education and health expanded very little and certainly less than in the 1970s. On the other hand 'business services' were not a particularly important sector in 1971, but went on to double their output from 1980 to 1990.

A large part of this increase in output comprises international services provided from London and the South East, where business services have already overtaken manufacturing in value of work. The sector increased its number of jobs (including the self-employed) by nearly 70 per cent from 1980 to 1990. Some other service sectors, including tourism, expanded their workforces by 20 to 40 per cent, but business services clearly outstripped the rest of the economy, including the public service sectors. In manufacturing, increased output per worker raised international competitiveness, but this productivity only reduced employment further, by nearly 23 per cent between 1980 and 1990, despite the increased output which is recorded in Fig. 7.1. We look at the growth of business services and tourism at a later stage in this chapter, but it is first necessary to assess a different kind of change in the 1980s.

## The role of small firms

The revival of small firms, as mentioned in Chapter 4, is a second most important distinctive feature of the 1980s. By the end of the decade firms employing fewer than ten people were creating roughly half the total net growth of jobs, despite employing less than one-fifth of all people. At the same time all the larger-sized premises were reducing the jobs provided.

Two principal reasons are normally given for the increased role of small firms in the 1980s. One was the supply of possible founders. This was based on the view that staff and workers made redundant from large industries would be induced to try and set up their own businesses rather than accept unemployment. A second reason was the increase in subcontracting. The 'farming out' of work from large firms to small was seen to explain a good part of the shift in the size distribution of establishments. In both cases, the effect would be to provide some compensation for the loss of jobs through 'de-industrialisation'. Many politicians saw the encouragement of small firms as the cornerstone of policies for reducing unemployment. It came to be widely believed that small firms contributed to regional development, partly through their own growth and partly through providing goods and services needed by larger firms.

Cambridge Science Park houses a number of small firms whose development has been the result of co-operation between commercial and research establishments.

Research for the European Commission has shown that small and medium-sized enterprises were increasing their role in the economy of most Community countries. The best measure to apply in the UK is a count of the total number of businesses registered for value-added tax (VAT). In the 1980s there was a large turnover in these businesses, with 14 per cent joining the total each year and 11 per cent de-registering. This difference yielded an overall increase of 33 per cent (420,000) in the number of UK businesses, 1980–90.

The crucial question is whether this source of growth reduced the north–south divide. There was certainly growth in small business everywhere. The percentage increase, however, varied between 12 per cent in parts of Wales and over 70 per cent in parts of the South East. At the regional level, Fig. 7.2 demonstrates a range of changes from 19 per cent in North West England to 46 per cent in the South East. All regions of the south expanded by more than 30 per cent, but none did so in the north. Thus Fig. 7.2 only underlines the impression from previous chapters of a *widening* north–south divide.

Two kinds of explanation have been offered for this pattern of change in small firms. The first is the availability of facilities: the south provides better access to finance and to technical information, and better opportunities for the recruitment of key staff. However, the second view stresses the larger proportions of potential business *founders* in the south; the greater *existing* population of small and medium-sized firms provides a 'seed-bed' containing many people who are capable of setting up a business on their own, whereas large northern factories may have none. A related reason for the leading position of the South East, East Anglia and the South West is their built-in structural advantage in starting the period with a greater share of the growing sectors run by small business. Production industries (including agriculture, mining and manufacturing) accounted for less than a tenth of the businesses and their growth. The outstanding field of expansion was the financial sector of small business, which more than doubled from 1980 to 1990, concentrated in London and the South East.

Fig.7.2 The increase of small business in the 1980s: percentage change in registrations for VAT, 1980–90.

*Source: Employment Gazette,* November 1991.

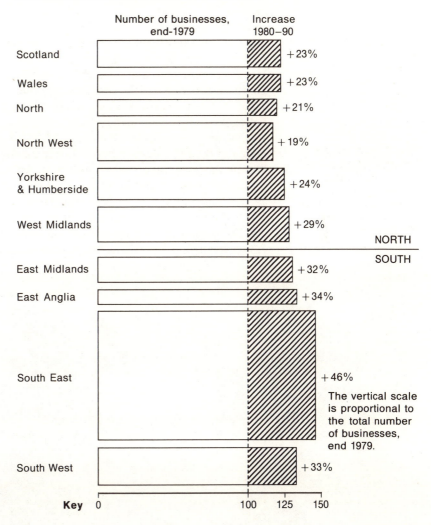

Number of businesses, end-1979    Increase 1980–90

Scotland +23%

Wales +23%

North +21%

North West +19%

Yorkshire & Humberside +24%

West Midlands +29%

NORTH

SOUTH

East Midlands +32%

East Anglia +34%

South East +46%

The vertical scale is proportional to the total number of businesses, end 1979.

South West +33%

Key    0    100    125    150

## Business services

The performance of their firms, both large and small, marks out business services as the outstanding focus of growth and geographical change in the 1980s. Traditionally the sector was best known for the activities of banking, insurance and finance, with three geographical arms: the institutions of the City of London; their networks of banks and building societies throughout the country; and the larger decentralised units, such as the credit card offices of Barclays in Northampton or Access in Southend. However, this section has been titled 'business services' because of the remarkable growth in the 1980s of a wider range of services. Many small offices sprang up providing computer software, management consultancy, recruitment advice, accountancy work, financial advice, market research and advertising.

The emergence of these growing sectors in a leading role represents a new level of specialisation in the British economy. To understand where they tend to locate, it is necessary to imagine both the linkages between them and the extent to which a company with a single national office must locate in London. The subsector comprising business services *other than* banking, insurance and finance expanded its employees by 657,000 between 1981 and 1989. In every region the rate of expansion exceeded 60 per cent, and in East Anglia the group more than doubled its staff. However, more than half the increase took place in London and the South East, because of the concentration there at the outset. There are some fields, such as market research, in which nearly 90 per cent of national offices remain in the region.

Returning to the larger employers in banking and insurance, the record of the 1980s demonstrates decentralisation both within and beyond the boundaries of the South East. Among the 15 leading relocations from central London in banking and insurance in the period 1983–87, four were to locations within Greater London, seven to the rest of the South East, three to the South West (at Gloucester, Poole and Bournemouth) and one to East Anglia (at Peterborough). Figure 7.3a combines all parts of the business services sector for 1981–89,

Fig.7.3 Percentage change in employment 1981–89, business services, including banking, insurance and finance: (a) by region, and (b) by county.

*Source:* NOMIS.

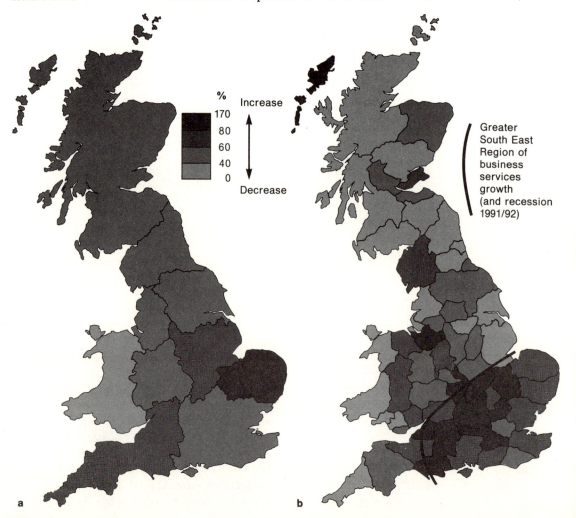

%   Increase
170
80
60
40
0
Decrease

Greater South East Region of business services growth (and recession 1991/92)

a

b

The Docklands development has attracted many thousands of jobs in the business services sector.

showing the greatest growth rate among employees in East Anglia, the South West and the East Midlands, because of this overspill from the South East. Most regions of the north exceeded a growth rate over 40 per cent, but this still fell below the national average.

A geographically more precise statement of the same trends is shown in Fig. 7.3b, which breaks down the data to county level. The remote west coast of Britain, together with six units of the east coast, show the poorest level of performance in employment change. The highest levels of growth, exceeding 80 per cent in eight years, occurred in the 'western arc', a semi-circle of counties from Surrey to Hertfordshire (South East), extending to Cambridgeshire (East Anglia), Northamptonshire (East Midlands), Warwickshire (West Midlands), and Dorset (South West) and along the M4 corridor to include Bristol (South West). There is also a significant area of growth in Cheshire (North West), which illustrates the importance of an attractive environment and access to an airport in all these trends.

London itself attracted nearly a quarter of a million jobs in business services, but as it started at a high level, this represented a percentage growth of only 40 per cent. Included in this total were the 20,000 jobs which had moved to the London Docklands development by 1988, following the reclamation of 600 hectares of derelict land. A further 8,000 jobs were expected to move to Docklands during 1991 and 1992, supported by renewed government investment in roads and infrastructure on a much greater scale than in Britain's other inner cities. Including therefore the 'western arc' and Docklands, the South East contains the greatest concentration of growth in this vital sector. As, however, the region's expansion has overflowed its conventional boundaries (Fig. 7.3a), it is more realistic to incorporate the other unshaded areas of Fig. 7.3b in an arc of greater radius drawn to represent a business services growth region of the greater South East (Fig. 7.3b). Its boundaries may expand and possibly contract according to future economic change, but there is little doubt about its emergence in the 1980s.

### The tourist industry

In those subregions which lacked the growth of business services, the promotion of tourism was often seen as the best means available for economic development in the 1980s. This might seem surprising when the traditional *seaside* resorts of older textbooks, such as Margate (Kent) or Morecambe (Lancashire), were struggling to maintain a role in the face of British holidaymakers' much increased use of foreign 'package holidays'. In fact the growth of second holidays and of day trips by the British, and of visits to Britain by foreigners, led to considerable growth of *inland* and of *urban tourism*. Examples of each follow below, but it is valuable first to view the overall structure of the British tourist industry (Fig. 7.4).

From 1980 to 1990, overseas residents' visits increased by 45 per cent, from 12.4 to 18.0 million, and their expenditure in Britain rose by 22 per cent. Spending by UK residents on holidays involving overnight stays increased moderately, even though the number of longer holidays decreased. However, spending on 'day trips' increased during the

A spell of good weather still brings holiday-makers to the beaches of traditional British seaside resorts, as here at Margate in Kent.

Fig.7.4 Tourism spending in the UK, 1990.

*Source: Employment Gazette,* September 1991.

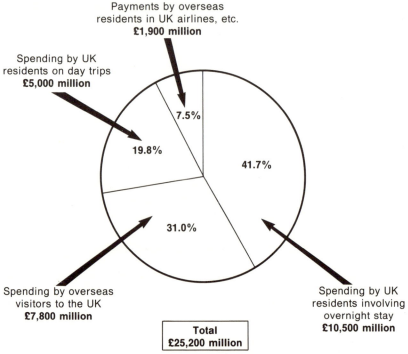

Payments by overseas residents in UK airlines, etc. **£1,900 million**

Spending by UK residents on day trips **£5,000 million**

**7.5%**

**19.8%**

**41.7%**

**31.0%**

Spending by overseas visitors to the UK **£7,800 million**

Spending by UK residents involving overnight stay **£10,500 million**

Total **£25,200 million**

decade as a result of the growth of car ownership and income and the reduction of working hours. They were estimated by 1990 to represent nearly 20 per cent of the tourist industry (Fig. 7.4).

Unfortunately the growing number of overseas visitors only adds to the advantage of London in the British economy. No less than 39 per cent of their nights in Britain are spent in the capital, and only 8 per cent, for example, in Scotland; through the 1980s the figures remained unchanged by efforts to spread more of this trade to the provinces. Only 5 per cent of tourist nights of British people, even including business and social visits, are spent in London. Figure 7.5a shows that overnight

Fig.7.5 Employment in tourism.
(a) Distribution of tourist nights of UK residents, 1990.

*Source:* United Kingdom Tourism Survey.

(b) Leading tourist attractions by numbers of visitors, 1989 (excluding cathedrals, churches and country parks).

*Source:* British Tourist Authority/English Tourist Board.

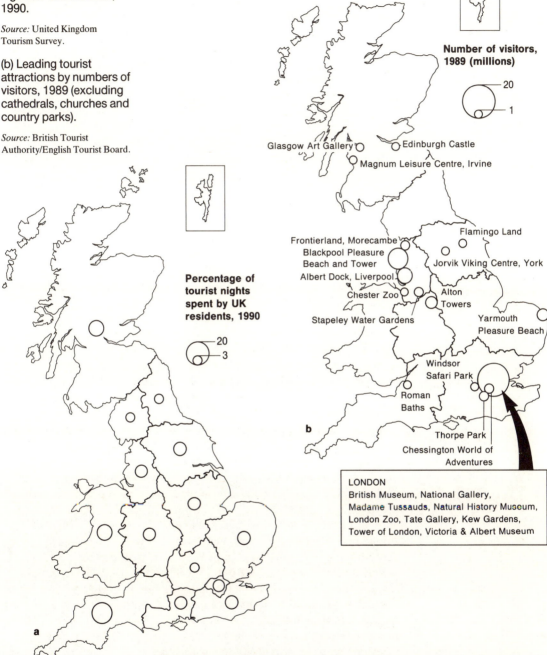

**Number of visitors, 1989 (millions)**

20
1

Glasgow Art Gallery    Edinburgh Castle
Magnum Leisure Centre, Irvine

**Percentage of tourist nights spent by UK residents, 1990**

20
3

Frontierland, Morecambe    Flamingo Land
Blackpool Pleasure Beach and Tower    Jorvik Viking Centre, York
Albert Dock, Liverpool
Chester Zoo    Alton Towers
Stapeley Water Gardens    Yarmouth Pleasure Beach

Windsor Safari Park
Roman Baths
b
Thorpe Park
Chessington World of Adventures

LONDON
British Museum, National Gallery,
Madame Tussauds, Natural History Museum,
London Zoo, Tate Gallery, Kew Gardens,
Tower of London, Victoria & Albert Museum

a

tourism is valuable in dispersing British spending away from the South East to support the economic base of other regions. The South West, with its large resorts of Bournemouth, Torbay, Newquay, and many smaller ones, attracted over 18 per cent of visitor nights in 1990. Rather disappointingly, Scotland and Wales attracted only 9 per cent each. The distribution of tourist nights by *region* has remained relatively stable over the last decade.

'Thrills and spills' at Alton Towers in Staffordshire attract day visitors from all over Britain.

## New forms of tourism

Changes in the structure of the tourist industry have none the less affected its geography. There is widespread evidence of stagnation in the trade of traditional coastal resorts. However, the growth of new forms of tourism was widely seen to offer growth prospects to inland areas and to the north of England, not only to their National Parks, but also to their urban and industrial areas. This view was based on the popularity of open-air parks such as Alton Towers in Staffordshire, and the Flamingo Land Zoo and Family Fun Park in North Yorkshire, and of attractions in urban industrial areas, such as the redeveloped Albert Dock, Liverpool, and the Glasgow Art Gallery. Figure 7.5b shows these to be among the leading 27 of the 1,815 'attractions' visited by 183 million people in 1989.

The evidence available in 1991 suggests, however, that the increase of tourism has been spread to a more varied range of destinations. A survey undertaken in 1988–89 identified 379 million visits extending over three hours and more than 40 miles (64 km) away from the home (Table 7.2). Over this distance, day tourism trips are particularly likely to affect economic geography by transferring expenditure between regions. Among the 379 million trips reported in Table 7.2 were 120 million spent on 'outdoor activities', followed by 57 million visits to 'attractions'.

Only about 16 per cent of the tourist trips in Britain were to the seaside. The pattern shows that no single kind of attraction has taken over from the traditional trip to the coastal resort. Despite all the emphasis on the scope for urban tourism, there is little evidence of a marked increase in tourism-related employment in the large cities, even in London. Much urban tourism remains concentrated on the more historic cities such as York or Bath. In all, 52.5 per cent of visits to tourist attractions in 1989 were to those in urban areas, but the greater growth of tourism employment in the 1980s was in rural areas.

It is possible to enumerate the number of employees in parts of the service sector related to tourism, although this inevitably reflects local as well as tourist use of restaurants, public houses, museums and sports centres. In all, these jobs expanded from 1.16 to 1.44 million between 1981 and 1991, an increase of 24.3 per cent. This was fairly evenly spread between the *regions*, though with the smaller increases in Scotland, the North and the North West. The pattern which emerges at *county* level is, however, one of relatively poor performances both in resort areas of the south coast (Dorset, the Isle of Wight and East Sussex) and in areas of de-industrialisation (South Yorkshire, north-east England, central Scotland and south Wales). The more attractive areas of the north of England, such as Cumbria, North Yorkshire and Cheshire, show growth above the average level. However, the greatest increases in this sector fell around the borders of the South East and of Wales. This area of increase represents the growth of residential population and income, spent in local restaurants and public houses, as well as of tourists. In general, therefore, it is apparent that, despite efforts to provide jobs for the school-leavers of northern cities in tourism and leisure industries, growth in the sector is tending to concentrate on rural areas and the south.

**Table 7.2  Leisure day-visits of more than 40 miles (64km), Great Britain 1988–89**

| Purpose of trip | Number of visits (millions) | Expenditure (£ millions) |
|---|---|---|
| Attractions, including: | 57 | 471 |
|    Park, garden, common | 8 | 130 |
|    Temporary show or carnival | 12 | 72 |
|    Zoo, aquarium, bird sanctuary, safari park | 10 | 62 |
|    Theme park | 7 | 43 |
|    Museum or art gallery | 6 | 50 |
|    Castle, ancient monument | 5 | 43 |
|    Stately home | 5 | 39 |
|    Cathedral or church | 2 | 15 |
|    Historic ship or steam railway | 2 | 17 |
| Outdoor activities, including: | 120 | 811 |
|    Taking part in outdoor sport | 13 | 325 |
|    General tour, sightseeing | 51 | 211 |
|    Walking, hiking, rambling, climbing | 12 | 85 |
|    Swimming, sunbathing | 11 | 47 |
|    Watching outdoor sport | 16 | 60 |
|    Fishing | 5 | 35 |
|    Picnicking | 6 | 4 |
|    Horse riding or pony-trekking | 1 | 18 |
|    Canoeing, rowing, sailing, windsurfing | 3 | 18 |
|    Power or motor-boating, water-skiing | 1 | 8 |
| Party, celebration, anniversary | 12 | 96 |
| Dance or disco | 5 | 56 |
| Visits or meetings with friends or relatives | 91 | 422 |
| Theatre, opera, cinema, ballet, concert | 13 | 166 |
| Bingo or casino | 0 | 1 |
| Public house or wine bar | 5 | 44 |
| Restaurant or café | 11 | 157 |
| Taking part in indoor sport | 5 | 32 |
| Watching indoor sport | 1 | 4 |
| Shopping trip (not routine) | 36 | 880 |
| Other | 24 | 218 |
| Total | 379* | 3,358 |

*The total of individual entries exceeds the actual total owing to rounding of decimal figures.

*Source:* Leisure Day Visits Survey, 1988/89, from *Employment Gazette* May 1991.

## Manufacturing growth industries

This chapter has so far considered the growth of parts of the service sector as the prime feature of the 1980s. It should not be forgotten, however, that there were some sectors of manufacturing which were running against the trend of decline of the decade. It is necessary to ask whether they amend the pattern so far reported. Nearly all major parts of the manufacturing sector showed a recovery from the recession of the early decade and contributed to an increase of output of 3.8 per cent per year between 1985 and 1990. The problem was, as mentioned in Chapter 5, that output per worker increased significantly faster than output. If manufacturing industry is divided into 210 parts, then only 57

of them showed an increase in employment from 1981 to 1989. These 57 tended to be in newer products such as plastics, in certain building and house-fitting materials and in parts of electronics, rather than in the 'heavy manufacturing' or 'metal-using industries' as enumerated in Chapter 5.

*Electronic growth industries*

This section is about just four of the 57 growth industries, and these four are the only examples of growth among the 16 parts of electrical and electronic engineering. Contrary to many impressions, and to its performance abroad, electrical and electronic engineering remained a significant contributor to job loss during the 1980s. That detracted from the record of 'high-technology industry' as a whole and led to manufacturing job loss in the M4 corridor from London to Bristol. What was growing in that corridor was, as we have seen, the business services group, including computer services.

The types of factory in the four groups have a lot in common other than their growth record. They make electronic consumer goods, electrical instruments and control systems, and security alarms. As a whole, they are an important example of industrial growth as they expanded employment by 52 per cent in the eight years 1981–89. In the past, industries of this kind often had their origins in London and the South East. The remarkable feature of their recent pattern of change was that the South East showed the smallest rate of increase – 5.7 per cent between 1981 and 1989. This in turn concealed reductions in Greater London and the adjoining counties of Surrey and Hertfordshire. Outside the South East, growth was greatest in the East Midlands and West Midlands, including dispersal towards Lincolnshire and Wales, although most northern regions also enjoyed an above-average rate of increase. This pattern confirms the recent tendency towards the 'de-industrialisation' of the South East. Expanding industries needing much labour could not compete with the growth of business services but looked rather to the adjoining regions or to the New Towns and 'assisted areas' of the north, especially at the end of the decade.

*Foreign direct investment*

Just as British industry as a whole reduced its employment, though with exceptions, so too did the foreign-owned factories that are located within Britain. Between 1981 and 1989 their employment fell by 17.2 per cent, but not in all regions or ownerships. There was heavy 'de-industrialisation' in foreign-owned factories, especially in the South East, but also some growth in three other regions of England.

One of these was the Northern Region, to which 105 manufacturing firms moved in the 1980s, creating 15,000 jobs. Of these, 76 per cent were generated by foreign companies, including no less than 40 per cent from the Far East (Fig. 7.6), notably the Japanese Nissan car factory and electronics firms from South Korea. However, there were also closures of foreign-owned plants in this period, both in the Northern Region and throughout the country. Thus, while the number of Japanese factory businesses in the UK jumped from 19 in 1981 to 89 in

The Japanese Nissan car company established a large factory in Sunderland during the 1980s.

1989, the number owned by United States companies fell from 1,510 to 1,058.

The conclusion to this chapter must be that while expansion was the norm in the 1980s in most service activities, it had become very much the exception in manufacturing. When the focus is on *recent change* since 1981, the prime movers of economic expansion and contraction are in the service sector. It is therefore increasingly important for the geographer to think of the future of his/her area as being determined by 'business' and not just by 'industry'. The growth businesses of the 1980s, especially among small firms, tended to thrive and expand most in four regions of the south. However, within both the north and the south, the introduction in this chapter of a map for counties (Fig. 7.3b) has demonstrated significant differences between urban and rural areas.

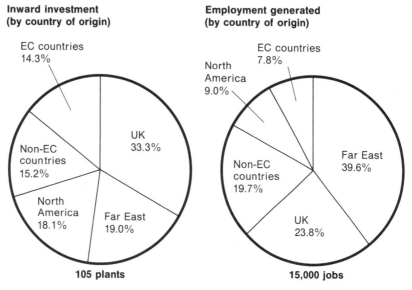

Fig.7.6 New factories in north-east England, 1980–90.

*Source:* Department of Employment.

# 8  Urban–rural contrasts in the 1980s

As the 'post-industrial' era develops, there is little doubt that the British people are returning to live in the countryside. The net movement of people is everywhere from counties of higher density, in terms of resident people per square kilometre, to counties of lower density. This migration is important for the kind of analysis undertaken in this book.

One reason for people's migration to rural counties is the growth of jobs there. In the maps of employment change at regional level in Chapters 5–7, the principal distinction was between northern and southern regions, especially in questions like the growth of small firms. However, in the south there was a persistent tendency for East Anglia, accompanied frequently by the East Midlands and the South West, to grow more than the South East. In the north, it was a repeated feature for North West England to perform worse than, say, Yorkshire and Humberside, or Wales. Perhaps the sharpest contrast is the one between East Anglia and the North West, the former increasing its population by 20.3 per cent between 1971 and 1991, and the latter falling by 7.0 per cent.

Such contrasts in production growth certainly reflect regional location – East Anglia lies in the south and the North West in the north. It may also be, however, that one is more rural than the other. In the nineteenth century, East Anglia had experienced de-industrialisation through the loss of its wool manufacturing industry, and the loss of farming jobs increasingly added to migration from the countryside and the region. Rural–urban migration became most significant. On the other hand, the smaller area of North West England was an area of attraction, which by 1921 attained 16 per cent of Great Britain's population through the growth of industry.

Especially since the war, the relationship has been reversed. To move to East Anglia became highly fashionable in the social climate of the 1980s, so much so that it attracted increasing numbers of people both for retirement and to seek jobs in its buoyant economy. On the other hand, the record levels of depopulation in North West England reflected net outward flows of retired people to the Lake District, Wales and the South West, and the facts of high unemployment, especially on Merseyside. These in turn reflected the image of an outworn urban environment of closely-spaced towns and industrial, working-class settlements.

East Anglia comprises a collection of some of the most favoured rural counties: Cambridgeshire, Norfolk and Suffolk. The North West incorporates two former metropolitan counties, Greater Manchester and Merseyside, together with Lancashire and Cheshire. Of these, only Cheshire shares any of the environmental and social features which have proved attractive for growth in the 1980s (Chapter 7). It may be, therefore, that the fundamentals of population growth and decline in

Astley Park near Chorley in Lancashire was built to provide new homes in a pleasant environment, away from congested city centres.

the two regions are closely related to the fact that one has a rural and the other an urban settlement pattern. If one wished to predict the relative growth or decline of different regions such as these, it might be possible to do so by studying their varying mixtures of urban settlements (liable to decline), and rural areas (liable to increase), as elsewhere in Britain.

This is to say, following the work of Fothergill and Gudgin (1982), that their inherited *geographical* structure has become more important for understanding regional growth than their *industrial* structure, which was paramount until the early post-war period. The strong national growth of rural population began in the early 1960s, and peaked in 1974 before continuing at a fairly high level, especially in the buoyant conditions of the 1980s. Remarkably, this tendency towards urban decline and rural growth in population became dominant in the 1970s in most developed countries, and geographers have named it 'counter-urbanisation'.

## Counter-urbanisation

It is clear that changes in the British distribution of population have been merely part of a universal pattern in the developed countries of the world. East Anglia and North West England have their counterparts in different areas of the USA, for example. A reversal of migration trends toward urban areas was first observed in the USA in the early 1970s, when estimates showed population to be growing faster in the non-metropolitan than in the metropolitan counties. It was found that depopulation was accelerating in the large cities and older industrial areas of the North East and the 'manufacturing belt', while industry, services and people were moving to smaller towns and to the less developed southern and western states.

Studies of censuses showed that the rates of population loss met by the large cities of most developed countries increased between the 1960s and 1970s, while the more rural areas frequently increased their population by net in-migration, thus reversing many decades of depopulation. Examples were found not only in Canada and Australia, but also in the more densely populated and smaller countries of Western Europe and even Japan. These features prompted people to think that the human map was changing in a manner as fundamental as in the Industrial Revolution.

This suggestion gained force from evidence of changes in the organisation of production and the distribution of employment. In industry and offices it became increasingly possible to separate head office functions, retained in the cities, from branch plants and 'back offices' which did the routine work. These could, as seen earlier, be established in areas with lower land and labour costs. Small firms could establish themselves in many rural zones of developed countries, and there was evidence that some professional workers, using personal computers, could do most of their work from 'tele-cottages' in rural areas.

If the underlying economic factors tended to attract firms to rural areas and repel them from urban ones, they were also reinforced by social factors. Not only in the USA but also elsewhere, the concentration of poorer and coloured minority groups in inner cities deterred white investment, while rural locations could be seen as free from all the past struggles, over workers' rights and pay, of industrialism. For these kinds of reason there was a change in the 'residential preferences', the desired living environment, of business, working and retired people. The growth of social welfare payments, private pensions and other benefits made it easier for people to move to the countryside, especially at the point of retirement from work. Additionally, improvement in transport, education, health and personal services could also contribute to a more equal role for rural areas in modern society. It is fairly easy to name these probable causes of the international trend towards 'counter-urbanisation', but more difficult to identify the most important ones at a given place and time.


**Census results for Great Britain**

Before looking at causes in Britain, it is clear that the effects of changes in population distribution are very consistent. Virtually the whole of Great Britain has been strongly affected by counter-urbanisation, whether in the form of urban depopulation or rural growth. In the quarter century to 1991 the trend has admittedly been checked during recessions, but it has always resumed its full vigour.

The effects can be seen first in regional population trends. The preliminary results of the 1991 census of population are mapped in Fig. 8.1a. As expected, East Anglia (+7.7%) and the North West (−4.3%) provided the most extreme difference between regions in the period 1981 to 1991, a total of 12.0 percentage points (7.7 + 4.3). However, like maps of employment change presented earlier (Fig. 6.6b, for example), the overall shape is far from a straightforward north–south division. For instance, the South East and Wales shared a very small reduction in total population.

Table 8.1 compares these data with employment trends for 1981–91 and with a measure of urban and rural character: the density of population in each region, expressed in terms of persons per square kilometre. It

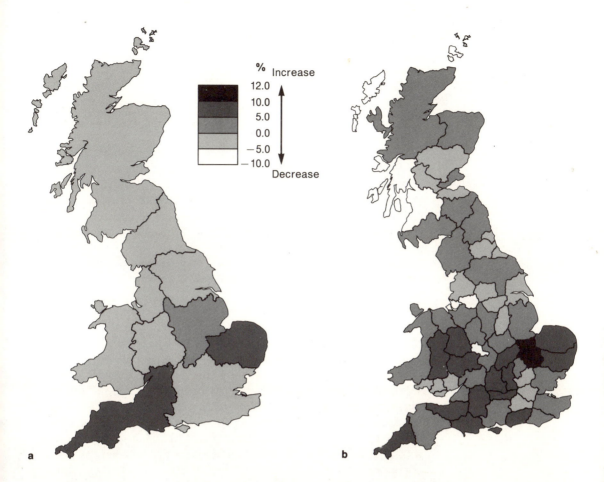

Fig.8.1 Change in total population in Great Britain, 1981–91: (a) by region, (b) by county.

*Source:* Preliminary results of the Census of Population 1991.

**Table 8.1    Principal trends by regional density of population, percentage change 1981–91 (June)**

|  | Persons per km² 1989 | Percentage change 1981–91 | |
| --- | --- | --- | --- |
|  |  | Population | Employment |
| **South** | | | |
| South East | 639 | 0.1 | +1.1 |
| East Midlands | 256 | +2.5 | +4.2 |
| South West | 195 | +5.5 | +11.8 |
| East Anglia | 163 | +7.7 | +17.3 |
| **North** | | | |
| North West | 870 | −4.3 | −4.5 |
| West Midlands | 401 | −1.4 | −1.4 |
| Yorkshire & Humberside | 320 | −1.8 | +1.5 |
| Northern Region | 200 | −3.0 | −2.8 |
| Wales | 138 | −0.0 | +2.6 |
| Scotland | 66 | −3.4 | −2.1 |

*Note:* The types of district shown in Fig. 8.2 demonstrate a maximum range of population change between 6.1 per cent for 'remoter, mainly rural districts' and −8.7 per cent for 'metropolitan principal cities' 1981–91. They demonstrate a maximum range of employment change between 16.8 per cent for 'remoter, mainly rural districts' and −6.8 per cent for 'metropolitan principal cities' 1981–89.

*Source:* Census of Population, *Employment Gazette* 1991.

85

becomes apparent, firstly, that it is the effects of counter-urbanisation which rule out any idea of an absolute 'north–south divide'. The gradual depopulation of London, whose presence in the region is registered in its measure of density, drags down the record of the South East. Two northern regions of lower density, Yorkshire and Humberside and Wales, showed a greater increase in employment between 1981 and 1991, than did the South East.

A second feature is not only that the South East ranks the highest and East Anglia the lowest within the south in terms of density of population, changes in population and changes in employment, but that the East Midlands and South West lie in second and third positions on all three measures. This regularity suggests the classic feature of counter-urbanisation, namely that growth is inversely related to the density of population. In the north, however, the same degree of regularity is spoilt by features discussed in other chapters, the effects of its industrial structure and location during a period of de-industrialisation.

In addition to producing results by county (Fig. 8.1b), the Office of Population Censuses and Surveys (OPCS) has addressed the issue by classifying the districts of England and Wales into 13 groups. The sharpest contrast in the 1980s population trends lay between the 'metropolitan principal cities', such as Birmingham, Manchester and Sheffield, and the 'remoter, mainly rural districts', which include areas such as North Dorset, West Derbyshire or Hambleton. As shown in the notes to Table 8.1, the difference in population trends between these groups amounted to 14.8 percentage points (6.1 + 8.7), compared with 12.0 (7.7 + 4.3) as noted earlier for the extreme pair of regions.

Fig.8.2 Percentage change in population by type of district, England and Wales 1981–91.

*Source:* Office of Population Censuses and Surveys, *1991 Census Preliminary Report for England and Wales*, Series CEN 91 PR (HMSO, London, 1991).

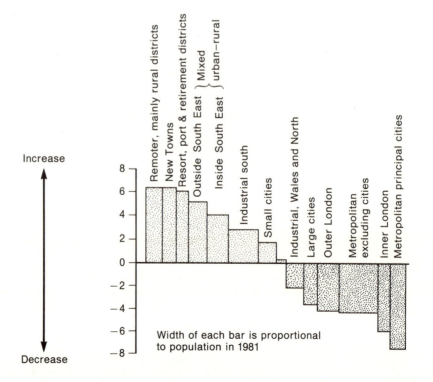

Figure 8.2 presents data for all 13 groups of district, as arranged by OPCS to provide a gradation between the two extremes in population trends. Clearly, London and the metropolitan districts, followed by large cities and industrial areas, account for the bulk of the decline in population, while increases become progressively greater as one moves towards more rural areas of lower density. In the employment record, the same gradation does not hold precisely, as jobs in more rural areas clearly expanded at a much faster rate than population in this time span. This was partly because the labour shortage of the Greater South East was met by more people, especially women, going out to work, rather than through additional house building and inward migration. Although no New Towns were started in this period, the pre-existing ones, such as Milton Keynes or Peterborough, were very important in attracting growth.

The most rapidly-growing areas were the 'remoter, mainly rural districts'. As shown by Fig. 8.2, if all these areas expanded their population in a consistent way it would go a long way towards explaining the population record of East Anglia, the South West and even Wales. In fact this group has experienced significant growth in every standard region, with only a few of its districts, mainly in Scotland, still suffering net population decline. A large number of these districts benefited from the growth of retirement population, tourism, service and even factory employment.

**Explanations for British counter-urbanisation**

It is necessary to ask which extreme, the city or the remote country, holds the best clues to understanding this re-distribution of people and jobs. On the whole, the starting point of the process is best seen in the urban areas, such as London and Manchester, and in forces of 'deglomeration'. London, but not the other cities, has been found to be a high-cost location for industry, partly on account of skilled labour shortages. More generally, however, the requirements of industry have outgrown the limits of urban sites. The increased use of machines meant on the one hand that the number of workers per thousand square metres of factory floor space fell, from 36.0 in 1964 to 21.4 in 1982, while on the other hand it was very difficult to find space to increase output at factory sites in built-up areas. Total employment would automatically fall unless the firm chose to relocate to an area with more room for expansion and better living conditions. What happened in conurbations was that the closure and contraction of plants was rarely offset by any commensurate growth of new firms. Thus from 1981 to 1989, factory employment fell by more than 30 per cent in both London and 'metropolitan principal cities', while it actually grew in just one group of districts, the 'remoter, mainly rural'. By the end of the decade these latter areas had increased their dependence on industry to a level close to the national average.

This book has shown how offices and service employment have decentralised from city centres over increasingly long distances. Many of these moves have occurred at times when national investment was at its peak. After the difficult economic conditions of the early 1980s there were pent-up pressures for housing and mobility, which could not be met in inner-city areas because of the progressive using up of sites there.

The recovery of the economy was so dominated by high-level service-sector jobs in central London that development costs and house prices were unprecedentedly high for miles around. This gave an extra push to railway commuting from stations as distant as Bournemouth, Swindon, Peterborough and Cambridge, beyond the boundaries of the South East, and set up chain movements which worked their way across the types of district of Fig. 8.2, eventually to deliver new factories and migrants to remoter, rural areas of the north.

The role of the individual is more than usually apparent in movement to rural areas. The decision of a couple to sell their house in an urban area and move to the countryside is important in increasing the retired population, which is well above the national average in counties such as Cornwall. However, the role of retirement migration in the urban–rural drift has sometimes been exaggerated. In Cornwall and most other rural counties the inflow of middle-aged people of working age is more important. Some may be factory owners, but others may set up or take over small businesses such as guest houses, caravan and chalet sites, cafés, restaurants and shops. Some service occupations in rural areas may suffer from the centralisation of activities like banks and secondary schools in towns, but they have gained from expansion in tourism, second homes and the retirement population. Thus regions such as South West England and Wales, other than the former mining valleys, are expanding through the re-distribution of wealth and of businesses which were initially created elsewhere.

**Summary: different scales of uneven development**

Such findings from the 1980s all require some recasting of the questions asked about geographical change in Britain. The simplest division of the country is between predominantly urban and predominantly rural areas. That is one which cuts across the standard regions which were defined at the beginning of this book. In the 1970s it was appreciated that large urban areas had similar problems of de-industrialisation, depopulation and poverty, *wherever* they happened to be located across the map of Britain. Equally, the 1970s demonstrated a remarkable revival of population growth in rural areas of England, Scotland and Wales.

The 1980s, however, have demonstrated the merits of making an additional division between northern and southern regions; London, the main city of the south, was slower than northern cities in losing population and employment, whereas the south's rural areas showed more rapid growth than did those of the north. The resulting fourfold division is used in Fig. 8.3, which provides a memorable summary of more detailed material on changes in employment.

The outstanding growth area, on this basis, is the 'rural south', extending across large parts of the South West, the South East, East Anglia and the East Midlands. It has more in common with the 'rural north' than with the 'urban south', although it clearly exceeds that area in importance and in rates of growth. The 'urban south' differs from the 'urban north' in showing a marginal gain in jobs rather than marginal losses. However, as urban conditions predominate more heavily in the northern regions, it is their different mixture of area characteristics which principally explains the 'north–south divide'.

Fig.8.3 Summary of percentage change in employment by type of district 1981–89.

*Source:* NOMIS.

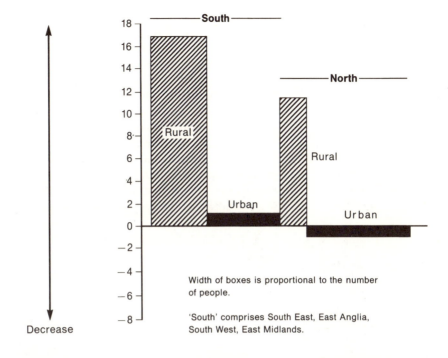

Width of boxes is proportional to the number of people.

'South' comprises South East, East Anglia, South West, East Midlands.

The construction site of the Channel Tunnel, near Dover. The Channel Tunnel will almost certainly help to continue the trend of uneven development between the north and the south.

The final measure of uneven development in this book is the rate of unemployment; that is, the number of people seeking work in an area divided by the total workforce, multiplied by 100. Such figures reflect the gap between job provision and labour supply. They are very important because they have many connections with the map of poverty. The rates of unemployment shown in Fig. 8.4 are for mid-1992, but the shape of the map is surprisingly persistent, even though at mid-1992 rates in the south had tended to converge with those in the north during a difficult economic recession. As would be expected from many maps presented throughout this volume, the lowest rate of unemployment was found in East Anglia (Fig. 8.4a) followed by the other regions of the south. In the rest of the country, the Northern Region suffered the worst rates of joblessness.

Fig.8.4 Percentage rate of unemployment, mid-1992:
(a) by region, (b) by county.

*Source:* NOMIS.

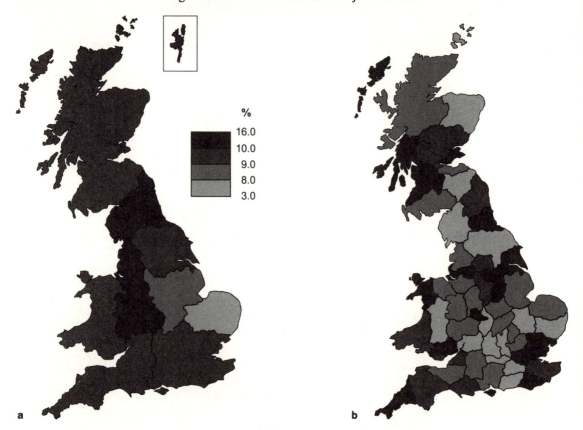

%
16.0
10.0
9.0
8.0
3.0

a

b

However, Fig. 8.4b reflects urban–rural variations of prosperity, many of them indicated by the previous county map (Chapter 7). In terms of unemployment, as of population and employment, there are commonly greater differences between the centre and periphery *within* each region than between the *average* prosperity of a given region and that of its neighbours. This does not complicate the understanding of geography too much if one is reminded that different regions contain different mixtures of urban and rural areas. For example, the urban conditions of Bristol or Norwich do not pull down the prosperity of the South West or East Anglia, respectively, as much as London frequently pulls down that of the South East. In the rest of the country, regional differences are still important. The map shows high levels of unemployment in the former metropolitan counties of the West Midlands, South Yorkshire, West Yorkshire, Greater Manchester, Merseyside and Tyne and Wear. It is argued that one reason for the greater prosperity of the East rather than the West Midlands is that there is a conurbation in the West, but none in the East. One reason for the deteriorating position of North West England lies in its inclusion of two large conurbations, Greater Manchester and Merseyside.

The regions of Britain will remain important building blocks in geographers' analyses. In the course of this book it has been valuable to reflect changing conditions in this century in terms of two successive broad divisions:

1 the 'axial belt' versus the 'peripheral region'
2 the 'north–south divide'.

It is best now to add an urban–rural distinction within the 'north' and within the 'south', lending primacy to the 'rural south' as the main growth region of the 1980s.


## Conclusion: policies for change

There are many arguments why governments and the European Commission should attempt to change the course of regional development. As has been shown, one strategy which was pioneered in the UK was to encourage the movement from 'core' to 'peripheral' regions – that is, from the 'axial belt' to the other coalfields. The 'regional policy' was useful in illuminating the problem, but it was pursued spasmodically. From the 1970s onwards it was less effective, while in the 1980s its principal significance was only in attracting foreign investment to Britain, for instance the Japanese plants, and encouraging such investment to go to Wales or the Northern Region. Much will depend on whether new governments of the 1990s do anything to revive the tools of regional policy, to extend or amend the 'assisted areas' of 1984 (Fig. 8.5), or establish elected assemblies for Scotland, Wales or regional government in England.

In individual problem areas, inner cities, steel closure areas, or outer rural districts, geographers are contributing to the thinking of mixed teams from different professions and agencies. In the 1980s, central government increasingly replaced its regional policy spending with the promotion of more local projects, in much the same way that this chapter has recognised the importance of marked variations between the districts of regions. This has meant that a variety of new grants and subsidies are available for local voluntary and business organisations to come together with government staff for a practical local objective. The welding together of these different interests is similar to geographers' aim of seeking to integrate understanding of different aspects of life in the same place.

Above the regional level, the European Community is aware of the probably harmful effects of the increased integration of trade across national boundaries on peripheral regions, such as those of northern Britain, and has taken steps to offset them in its own support of regional and related policies. The Community will increasingly affect the geography of Britain through its interest in environmental standards and its requirements for the thorough assessment of major projects before they are built. Whether these projects are industrial, port, airport or road developments, they are scrutinised for all their geographical implications in a way unheard of when the British built environment as we know it was developed.

Fig.8.5 Regional policy: assisted areas from 1984.

*Source:* Department of Trade and Industry.

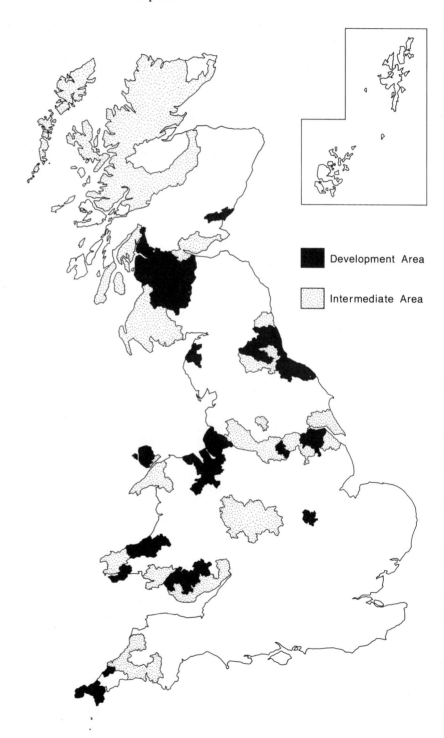

Development Area

Intermediate Area

# Sources and bibliography

There is a large and expanding literature relating to the regional development of Britain. Selected books and sources are entered below under their most appropriate chapter. The first section of this bibliography concentrates on recent texts, including contributions from related disciplines such as economics and politics.

## General texts

**Armstrong, H. and Taylor, J.** (1985) *Regional Economics and Policy*, Philip Allan, Oxford.

**Balchin, P. N.** (1990) *Regional Policy in Britain: the North–South Divide*, Paul Chapman, London.

**Champion, A. G., Green, A. E., Owen, D. W., Ellin, D. J. and Coombes, M. G.** (1987) *Changing Places: Britain's demographic and social complexion*, Edward Arnold, London.

**Champion, A. G. and Townsend, A. R.** (1990) *Contemporary Britain: a geographical perspective*, Edward Arnold, London.

**Clout, H.** (1986) *Regional Variations in the European Community*, Cambridge University Press, Cambridge.

**Cooke, P.** (ed.) (1989) *Localities: the changing face of urban Britain*, Unwin Hyman, London.

**Damesick, P. and Wood, P.** (eds) (1987) *Regional Problems, Problem Regions, and Public Policy in the United Kingdom*, Oxford University Press, Oxford.

**Hudson, R. and Williams, A.** (1986) *The United Kingdom*, Harper and Row, London.

**Johnston, R. J. and Gardiner, V.** (eds) (1991, 2nd edn) *The Changing Geography of the United Kingdom*, Methuen, London.

**Lever, W. F.** (1987) *Industrial Change in the United Kingdom*, Longman, Harlow.

**Lewis, J. and Townsend, A.** (eds) (1989) *The North–South Divide*, Paul Chapman, London.

**Martin, R. and Townroe, P.** (eds) (1992) *Regional Development in the British Isles in the Nineteen Nineties*, Jessica Kingsley, London.

**Prestwich, R. and Taylor, P.** (1990) *Introduction to Regional and Urban Policy in the United Kingdom*, Longman, London.

**Smith, D.** (1989) *North and South: Britain's economic, social and political divide*, Penguin, Harmondsworth.

## Chapter 1

**Central Statistical Office** (annual) *Regional Trends*, HMSO, London.
**Myrdal, G.** (1957) *Economic Theory and Underdeveloped Regions*,
Duckworth, London.
**Ordnance Survey** (1982) *The Ordnance Survey Atlas of Great Britain*,
144–77, Ordnance Survey, Southampton and Country Life Books,
Feltham.
**Watson, J. W. and Sissons, J. B.** (1964) *The British Isles : a systematic
geography*, Nelson, London.

## Chapter 2

**Bradford, M. and Kent, W. A.** (1977) *Human Geography: theories and
their applications*, Oxford University Press, Oxford.
**Hall, P.** (1976) 'England circa 1900', in **Darby, H. C.** (ed.) *A New
Historical Geography of England after 1600*, Cambridge University
Press, Cambridge.
**Marshall, M.** (1987) *Long Waves of Regional Development*, Macmillan,
Basingstoke.
**Massey, D.** (1984) *Spatial Divisions of Labour*, Macmillan, Basingstoke.
**Ward, S. V.** (1988) *The Geography of Interwar Britain : the state and
uneven development*, Routledge, London.

## Chapter 3

**Coates, B. E. and Rawstron, E. M.** (1971) *Regional Variations in
Britain: studies in economic and social geography*, Batsford, London.
**Hall, P.** (1982) *Urban and Regional Planning*, Penguin,
Harmondsworth.
**Law, C. M.** (1980) *British Regional Development since World War I*,
David & Charles, Newton Abbot.
**Prestwich, R. and Taylor, P.** (1990) *Introduction to Regional and Urban
Policy in the United Kingdom*, Longman, London.
**Townsend, A. R.** (1987) 'Regional policy', pp. 223–39 in **Lever, W. F.**
*Industrial Change in the United Kingdom*, Longman, Harlow.

## Chapter 4

**Holland, S.** (1976) *Capital versus the Regions*, Macmillan, Basingstoke.
**Lever, W.F.** (1987) *Industrial Change in the United Kingdom*, pp.
108–95, Longman, Harlow.
**Massey, D. B.** (1979) 'In what sense a regional problem?', *Regional
Studies* **13**, 233–43.
**Peck, F. W. and Townsend, A. R.** (1987) 'The impact of technological
change upon the spatial pattern of UK employment within major
corporations', *Regional Studies* **21**, 225–40.
**Watts, H. D.** (1987) *Industrial Geography*, Longman, Harlow.

## Chapter 5

**Fothergill, S. and Guy, N.** (1990) *Retreat from the Regions: corporate
change and the closure of factories*, Jessica Kingsley, London.
**Hudson, R. and Sadler, D.** (1989) *The Iron and Steel Industry :
restructuring, state policies and localities*, Routledge, London.

**Martin, R. and Rowthorn, B.** (eds) (1986) *The Geography of De-industrialisation*, Macmillan, Basingstoke.
**Massey, D. B. and Meegan, R. A.** (1982) *The Anatomy of Job Loss: the how, why and where of employment decline*, Macmillan, Basingstoke.
**Townsend, A. R.** (1983) *The Impact of Recession: on industry, employment and the regions*, Croom Helm, London.
**Townsend, A. R. and Peck, F. W.** (1985) 'The geography of mass redundancy in named corporations', pp. 174–218 in **Pacione, M.** (ed.) *Progress in Industrial Geography*, Croom Helm, London.

## Chapter 6

**Daniels, P.** (1982) *Service Industries: growth and location*, Cambridge University Press, Cambridge.
**Daniels, P.** (1985) *Service Industries: a geographical appraisal*, Methuen, London.
**Jones, Lang, Wootton Consulting and Research** (annual) *The Decentralisation of Offices from Central London*, Jones, Lang, Wootton, London.
**Marshall, J. N.** *et al.* (1989) *Uneven Development in the Service Economy : understanding the location and role of producer services*, Oxford University Press, Oxford.
**Price, D. G. and Blair, A. M.** (1989) *The Changing Geography of the Service Sector*, Belhaven, London.

## Chapter 7

**Baty, B. and Richards, S.** (1991) 'Results from the Leisure Day Visits Survey, 1988–89', *Employment Gazette* **99**, May, 257–68.
**Breheny, M. and Congdon, P.** (eds) (1989) *Growth and Change in a Core Region: the case of South East England*, Pion, London.
**Leyshon, A. and Thrift, N.** (1989) 'South goes north? The rise of the British provincial financial centre', in **Lewis, J. and Townsend, A.** *The North–South Divide*, Paul Chapman, London.
**Mason, C. M.** (1987) 'The small firm sector', pp. 125–48 in **Lever, W.F.** *Industrial Change in the United Kingdom*, Longman, Harlow.
**Townsend, A.** (1992) 'New directions in the growth of tourism employment? Propositions of the 1980s', *Environment and Planning A 24*, 821–32.

## Chapter 8

**Champion, A. G.** (ed.) (1989) *Counterurbanization, the Changing Pace and Nature of Population Deconcentration*, Edward Arnold, London.
**Fothergill, S. and Gudgin, G.** (1982) *Unequal Growth: urban and regional employment change in the UK*, Heinemann, London.
**Healey, M. J. and Ilbery, B. W.** (eds) (1985) *The Industrialization of the Countryside*, Geo Books, Norwich.
**Joshi, H.** (ed.) (1989) *The Changing Population of Britain*, Blackwell, Oxford.

# Index